CASINO GAMES

by Bill Friedman

GOLDEN PRESS • NEW YORK
Western Publishing Company, Inc.
Racine, Wisconsin 53404

FOREWORD

Casino Games is a guide to the five most popular games usually offered by casinos—Blackjack, Craps, Keno, Baccarat, and Roulette. They appear in the order of their popularity, and the text describes every bet currently offered throughout America in all the various locales. Each bet is explained in detail, including the location where each wager is made, the proper procedure for making it, the way dealers will handle each wager, the customary way dealers pay off each winning wager, and so on.

The author is grateful to the following professionals in the gaming industry for reading various chapters of the manuscript and recommending changes and improvements: Marty Carson, Tony Frabbiele, Jim Hall, Jim Gallagher, Art Luongo, Wayne McClure, Steve Miller, Howard Schwartz, and Joe Sewell.

This book is written in the memory of Mark Swain, who introduced me to the general editor and made possible the publication of the first edition.

I am most appreciative of my wife, Gladyce, for her loving support, encouragement, and patience during the writing and updating of this book.

BF

Revised and Updated Edition, 1996

 Produced in the U.S.A. by Western Publishing Company, Inc. Published by Golden Press, New York, N.Y. Library of Congress Catalog Card Number: 72-95510 ISBN: 0-307-24358-3

CONTENTS

INTRODUCTION

Casino gaming is rapidly becoming a popular form of recreation in many parts of the United States. The main object is to win money, but many people play just for fun and are not overly concerned about winnings. They may enjoy matching wits with the casino or trying to beat the "odds," the laws of probabilities. Gambling, which has been called a "love affair with chance," can be exhilarating but also very costly. No one should ever bet money he or she cannot afford to lose.

Casino Games teaches beginners the rules of the most commonly played games and describes the various betting situations, to help players get the most action from their available funds. Experienced casino customers can use this book to better understand the mathematical principles that govern each game, which are explained in the appropriate sections of this book. The novice might choose to quickly skim over or skip these rather difficult sections altogether.

Common gambling terms, which appear in many of the bet descriptions, are usually defined the first time they are used. They are included to help make readers feel more comfortable when entering a casino. Most of the illustrations in this book are patterned after the layouts used on the Las Vegas Strip. Some in the Craps section, however, more closely resemble the layouts used in Reno and Lake Tahoe.

Las Vegas is the gaming capital; more money is wagered there than in any other city in the world. Gaming jurisdictions across the country use variations of the rules Las Vegas uses. People interested in casino games can easily apply whatever they learn about gambling in Las Vegas to gambling in a casino on a riverboat, on land in another state, on a Native

American reservation, or in another country. The rules in Atlantic City are the most standardized because they were created by the state government, not casino operators, but all are based on Nevada rules as described in this book.

Perhaps the most important information in this book is the advice given on what are the best bets to make—the bets with the lowest "casino advantage" (see page 6). The casino advantage percentage is what generates a profit for the casino. In this guide every bet discussed includes this percentage so you can compare the relative merits of each game and the bets it offers.

A customer can wager either money or chips at any of the gaming tables in Nevada, but no cash may be wagered in Atlantic City and some other areas. The dealer always pays off winning wagers with chips worth $1, $5, $25, $100, $500, or sometimes even more. (You will learn from this guide how to buy chips at each of the games.) When a customer concludes play—hopefully a winner—the chips are usually taken to the cashier's cage, prominently located in the casino, and exchanged for regular currency.

Most casinos give complimentary cocktails to customers as they play Blackjack, Roulette, or Baccarat. The drinks are kept on the edges of the table in front of where the customers are playing. In Craps, drinks are served on a shelf that runs around the table; women can also place their handbags on this shelf.

Tipping the dealer is not mandatory, but many players do it. There are no set standards, so players must decide for themselves if, when, and how much to tip.

Some players make occasional small wagers for the dealer instead of tipping (players should always inform dealers when they are doing this); other players tip occasionally, either while playing or right before they leave the table. A tip is certainly in order if a dealer has been very helpful. On the other hand, if a dealer is rude or refuses to explain the casino's rules, the player should either move to another table or go to a casino where players are treated more courteously.

Casino Advantage

Casinos earn profits on each gambling transaction by charging a fee called the "casino advantage." This is the average percentage the casino takes out of each wager. Casino advantage can best be illustrated in the following coin-flipping scenario:

If you were to flip a coin against a hypothetical casino and wager $1 that every flip would be heads, you would lose $1 for every flip in which tails appeared. However, the casino would pay only 99¢ when you won (flipped a head). Thus you would win an average of only 99¢ for every $1 lost. You would be out an average of 1¢ for every two flips wagered and would lose 1¢ for every $2 invested. One cent is 0.5 percent (the casino advantage) of $2.

A casino expects to win the casino advantage percentage out of a customer's total "wagering handle"—the value of all a customer's wagers added together. For example, suppose a customer who buys $100 in chips wagers one $1 chip at a time; if the casino advantage in this example is 1 percent, the customer will make an average of 10,000 wagers to lose the $100 bankroll, because 1 percent of a wagering handle of $10,000 equals $100.

Even though players may wager only a small, finite number of times, they are still likely to experience a normal sampling of the statistical distribution. Thus large casinos especially, which generate so much business, almost always come away over the course of a year with the expected casino advantage percentage from their customers' total wagering handles.

The more wagers customers make, the less likely they will experience a deviant sample (i.e., a long winning streak) and the more likely they will lose an amount equal to the casino advantage percentage. More wagers also create a large wagering handle, which increases the casino's expected win.

Based on these two statistical principles, it is clear that customers who want to maximize their chances of winning should make as few wagers as possible. Ideally, customers should take all the money they intend to gamble during their lifetime and wager it at one time on the bet with the lowest casino advantage!

Many customers use one or more of the following three "systems" in a misguided attempt to alter the casino advantage:

- **Money Management.** There are many different theories and methods of money management. Some customers increase the size of their wagers when losing, trying to catch up. Others bet more when winning. But these methods have no statistical effect whatsoever on the casino advantage.

- **Incorrectly Applying the "Law of Averages."** For instance, 12 appears an average of once in every 36 rolls of the dice, so some customers assume that if 12 has not appeared for 100 rolls, it is then more likely to appear soon after. But the dice have no memory.

- **Combining Several Wagers on the Same Layout.** This is sometimes done in a futile attempt to alter the casino advantage. Some customers try to protect their money by balancing their wagers so that when one bet loses, another wins, etc. But the casino advantage stays the same for every individual bet, whatever the combination of wagers.

SLOTS
aler must draw to
INSURANC

BLACKJACK

In the game of Blackjack, also known as Twenty-One, the customer is not permitted to wager on all of the various alternatives. Specifically, the customer is not allowed to wager on the dealer's hand or on any of the other customers' hands. A player's only concern should be his or her hand in relation to the dealer's, since the other players' actions will have no appreciable effect on anyone else's winning or losing. The object in the game of Blackjack is for the player and dealer to get as close as is possible to a card count of 21 without going over. The one who gets closest to that point total wins.

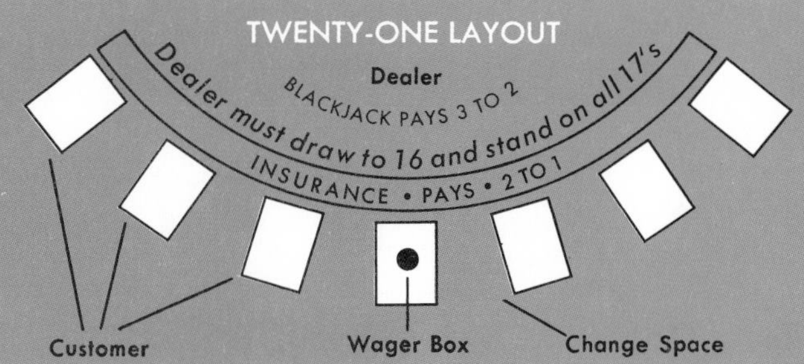

TO MAKE A WAGER, put it in the box in front of your chair. Wagers must be made before the first card is dealt and may not be touched after the first player has received his or her first card. If you want your currency changed into chips or the chips converted into another denomination, be sure to place them in the neutral zone between boxes to signify "change" or "no bet"; everything placed in a box is considered a wager. The dealer will not make change while a hand is in progress, except in those situations where you are allowed to add to your wager. At the end of the hand the dealer will place the change in front of you. Casinos in Nevada and some other places still allow customers to wager cash. When you place large bills in the wagering box in these casinos, the dealer will often ask, "Change or play?"

ALLOWABLE WAGERS are usually prominently displayed at each table along with other playing rules. The minimum wager may be $2, $3, or $5, although many casinos offer a lower than usual minimum during slower periods. Larger wagers may be permitted in increments of $1, but higher increments are more usual. Maximum wagers can vary quite a bit, depending on the type of casino. Smaller casinos may have a $500 maximum, but large, busy casinos may routinely offer a $5,000 maximum or even higher, sometimes up to many thousands of dollars.

CARD SUITS (Spades, Hearts, Diamonds, and Clubs) are not significant in this game and can be ignored. The point value of the cards determines the outcome. The cards 2 through 9 equal their face value. The 10's, Jacks, Queens, and Kings all have a value of 10. Aces can count as either 1 point or 11 points—it is up to the player. But you should always count an Ace as 11 unless the total value of your hand would exceed 21.

CARD VALUES

EACH CARD = FACE VALUE

EACH CARD = FACE VALUE

EACH CARD = 10 POINTS

AN ACE = 1 OR 11

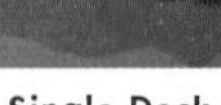

Single Deck

4-Deck Shoe

PLAYING THE GAME involves using anywhere from one to eight standard 52-card decks. If one or two decks are used, they are usually dealt by hand; more decks than this are almost always dealt from a device called a "shoe." But however the cards are dealt, the same playing rules apply.

THE DEALER offers the cut to a player after the cards are shuffled. Any player may refuse to cut the cards. If all do, the dealer makes the cut. The player should use only one hand to make a single cut toward the middle of the deck. The dealer will complete the cut. In all multiple-deck and many single-deck games, the dealer keeps possession of the shuffled deck and the player cuts it with a special "cut" card.

Cutting a Single Deck

Cutting a Multiple Deck

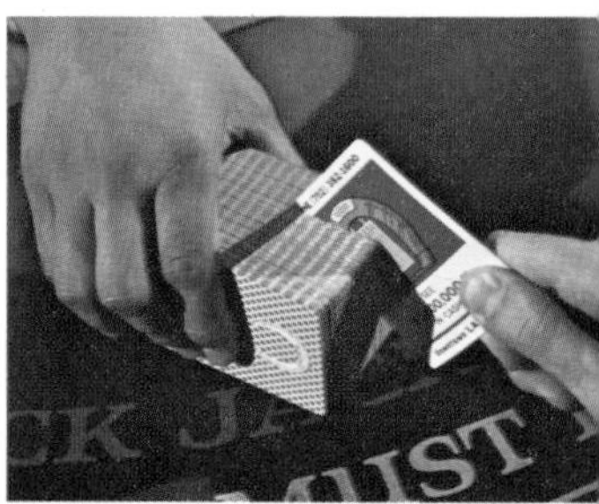

The Burn Card

THE "BURN" CARD refers to the first card, which the dealer removes from the deck. In a single-deck game, this card is placed face up on the bottom of the deck or face down in a discard tray. All the cards that are later used in the hand are discarded in the same way. The first and last cards in a deck are never used in a hand, even if the dealer runs out of cards during the hand. In this situation, the dealer must shuffle and continue dealing at the position of interruption. In general, the dealer can shuffle the cards at any point in the game except when a hand is in progress.

MULTIPLE BURN CARDS are used in many multiple-deck games. The dealer removes the first card from the shoe and turns it face up on the table. The point value of this card (2 to 10) determines the number of additional cards to be burned. The dealer removes the burn cards from the shoe and lays them face down on the table, then discards them. If the first burn card is a picture card (Jack, Queen, or King), ten more cards are burned. An Ace requires just one more burn card.

Alternative Method of "Burning"

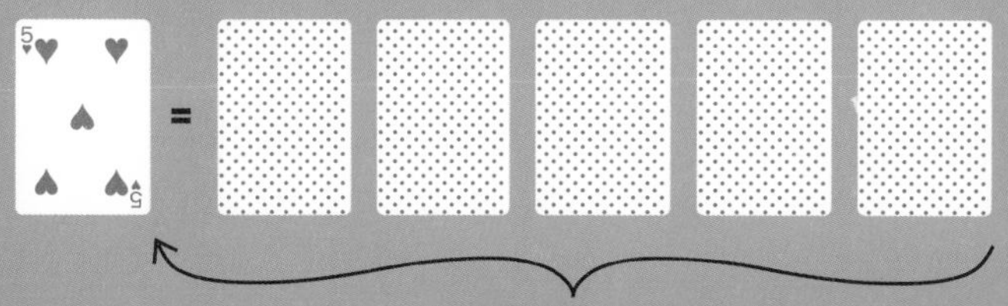

THE DEAL begins when all the players have finished making their wagers. The dealer starts with the player to the right, at "First Base" (see diagram below), and deals in a clockwise fashion. One card at a time is dealt to each player, with the dealer's card being dealt face up. Then a second card is dealt, with a "Hole" card being slid face down under the dealer's face-up card. The players immediately pick up their two cards and calculate their totals. You should always hold the two cards completely off the table in only one hand; this avoids accidentally bending them or removing them from the dealer's sight.

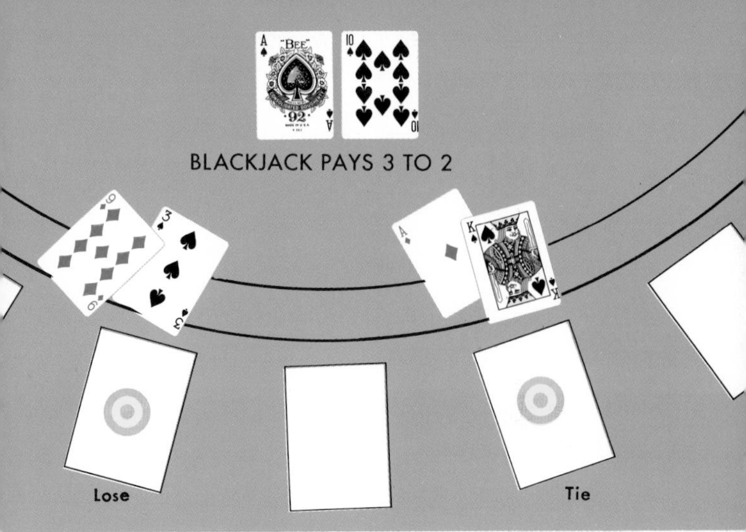

BLACKJACK occurs when the dealer's first two cards (an Ace and any 10-value card) total 21. In most casinos the dealer checks out the face-down card right away if the face-up card is either an Ace or worth 10 points. If the dealer has Blackjack, the Hole card is turned up and the hand ends. All players lose except those who also have Blackjack, which means a tie (also called a "push" or "standoff"). In this case, the player's wager is neither won nor lost. In some casinos, the dealer does not look at the Hole card, even when an Ace or a 10-point card shows, until all players have completed the hand. If the dealer has Blackjack, the players lose their initial wagers but are given back any wagers made after their original bet, for example, Double Downs and Splits (see pages 22 and 24). If the dealer doesn't have Blackjack, winning players lay their cards face up and receive a payoff of 3 to 2. All other bets except Insurance (see page 27) are paid 1 to 1.

PLAYERS "STAND" (indicate that they are satisfied with their hand and don't want to receive any more cards) by sliding the original two cards under the wager. This should always be done without touching the wager. The dealer then completes the hand in clockwise rotation, one player at a time, beginning with the player on the right side of the table (First Base). The dealer will stop only at those players who are still holding their original two cards.

A "HIT" is requested by those players who want to add cards to their hand to increase the total point count. Players who want a hit may brush the edge of their original two cards over the table or make a beckoning motion with their hand. The dealer will then place another card face up in front of the player on the dealer's side of the wager. After each hit, the player may continue to draw cards until the total count of the hand reaches or exceeds 21.

PLAYERS "BREAK" (lose) if they hit and their point total goes over 21. The player who breaks must immediately turn the original two cards face up and lay them on the dealer's side of the wager. The dealer takes the losing wager and places the player's cards in the discard tray. The dealer then continues dealing in a clockwise direction around the table until all the players have had a chance to complete their hands.

Face-up Dealing

FACE-UP DEALING is now practiced at many casinos. When the original two cards are dealt face up, players do not handle them. They obtain hits by scratching one or more fingers toward themselves next to their cards and stand by holding their open palm up to the dealer, who then proceeds to the next hand. Beginning players are better off playing at a table where the cards are dealt face up, since the dealer can give better advice if the cards are exposed. Because all dealers must play by fixed house rules, the player need not worry that the dealer's actions will be influenced by seeing the player's cards.

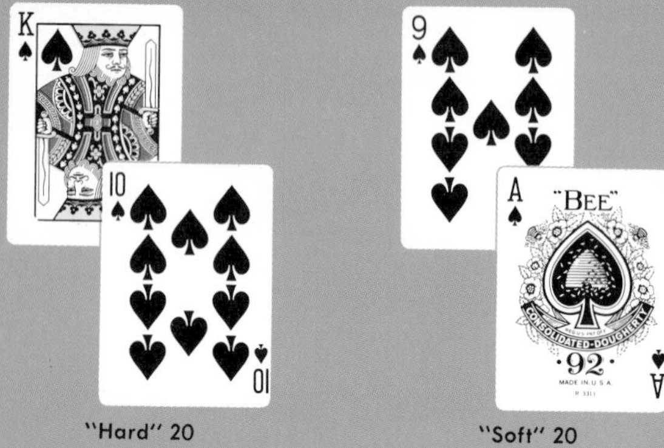

"Hard" 20

"Soft" 20

A HARD HAND either contains no Aces or each Ace is counted as 1.

A SOFT HAND contains one or more Aces, with the first Ace counted as 11 points. Previously it was noted that you should always count an Ace as 11 unless your total exceeds 21. If it does, you can then subtract 10 from your total, counting the Ace as only 1 point.

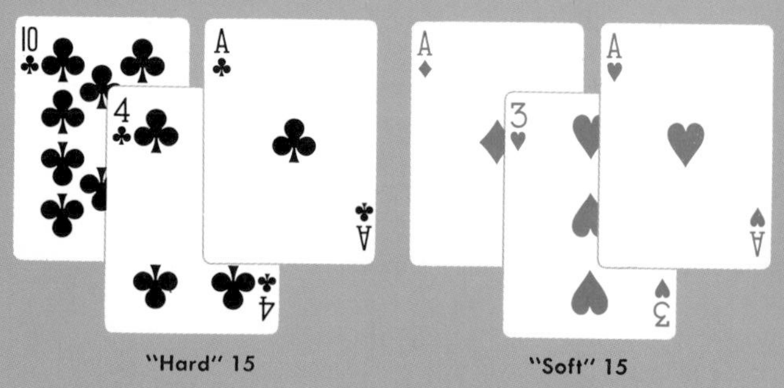

"Hard" 15

"Soft" 15

FIXED RULES are in force at most casinos. When all players' hands have been completed, the dealer's Hole card is turned up and the hand is played out according to "house rules." For example, the dealer must hit a Hard 16 or less and stand on a Hard 17 or over. All casinos stand on Soft 18 or over, and most follow the Las Vegas Strip rule of also standing on Soft 17—a slight advantage to the player. If the dealer goes over 21, he or she breaks and must pay off all wagers except those of players who have also gone over 21.

A WIN occurs when a player has a total count higher than the dealer's but not over 21. If the dealer stands with a count of 17 to 21 (a "Pat" hand), all players with a count higher than the dealer's but not above 21 are paid off. Those with a lesser total lose their wagers. If both the dealer and the player stand with the same total between 17 and 21, no money changes hands. The dealer indicates a tie and removes the player's cards but leaves the wager. This money remains for the next hand unless the wager is altered or the person quits playing and removes the wager.

THE BASIC STRATEGY for playing Blackjack has been determined by a number of computer experts; it is the correct strategy to use when discards have not been noted. The general principle behind the basic strategy is to balance the probability of a player's breaking against the probability of the dealer having a Pat hand (17 to 21). The player's action is based on the point count of the dealer's face-up card, which determines the probability of each type of total point count possible.

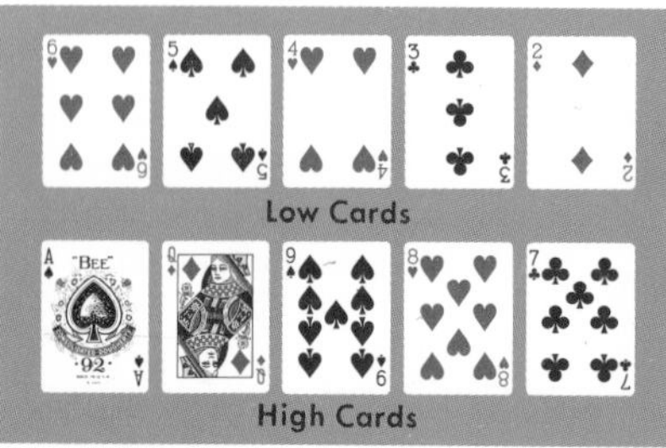

A STIFF is a total count of Hard 12 to Hard 16. You should always hit with a Hard total of less than 12 points. This is because your total count can increase with the next draw without any danger of it going over 21. Always stand with a Hard total of 17 or better, because you have a Pat hand. The only totals that you would hit and risk going over 21 are Hard 12 to Hard 16. You should decide whether to hit or stand on these totals based on the value of the dealer's face-up card presented in the Hard-hand hitting strategy that follows.

HARD-HAND HITTING STRATEGY is used when the player has Hard 12 to Hard 16. The player should hit all Stiffs, even though there is a risk of breaking when the dealer has a high face-up card of 7 to Ace. With a high face-up card, the dealer will probably end up with a Pat hand. When the dealer has a low face-up card of 2 to 6, he or she must hit to obtain the required minimum of Hard 17, even though there is a risk of breaking. In some casinos the dealer stands on Soft 17 and does not hit a 6 with an Ace in the Hole.

HARD-HAND HITTING STRATEGY

PLAYER	DEALER'S CARD 2	3	4	5	6	7	8	9	10	A
17	Stand	Stand	Stand	Stand	Stand	Stand	Stand	Stand	Stand	Stand
16	Stand	Stand	Stand	Stand	Stand	Hit	Hit	Hit	Hit	Hit
15	Stand	Stand	Stand	Stand	Stand	Hit	Hit	Hit	Hit	Hit
14	Stand	Stand	Stand	Stand	Stand	Hit	Hit	Hit	Hit	Hit
13	Stand	Stand	Stand	Stand	Stand	Hit	Hit	Hit	Hit	Hit
12	Hit	Hit	Stand	Stand	Stand	Hit	Hit	Hit	Hit	Hit

Stand
Hit

When the dealer has a low face-up card, the player should not hit a Stiff and risk "breaking." The only exception is when he or she has a Hard 12 and the dealer's face-up card is a 2 or a 3.

SOFT-HAND HITTING STRATEGY dictates that a player should always hit a Soft hand of 17 or less because these counts win only when the dealer breaks. The player risks giving up the occasional push (tie) when the dealer also has 17, but much more often the total is improved. The player should hit Soft 18 only when the dealer has a face-up card of 9 or 10. A player who hits and ends up with a Soft total of over 21 can subtract 10 to make it a Hard total of under 21.

SOFT-HAND HITTING STRATEGY

PLAYER	DEALER'S CARD 2	3	4	5	6	7	8	9	10	A
19	Stand	Stand	Stand	Stand	Stand	Stand	Stand	Stand	Stand	Stand
18	Stand	Stand	Stand	Stand	Stand	Stand	Stand	Hit	Hit	Hit
17	Hit	Hit	Hit	Hit	Hit	Hit	Hit	Hit	Hit	Hit

Stand
Hit

PROPOSITION BETS permit players to increase their wagers after they have seen their first two cards. The Proposition Bets are Double Down, Split Pairs, and Insurance. Rules may vary slightly in different casinos, but each table has a sign that lists the Proposition Bet rules as well as wager limits. The dealer can provide further clarification if needed.

Proposition Bets allow players to reduce their initial disadvantage. This disadvantage comes from those situations in which both the player and the dealer break. In these cases, the player loses; it is not considered a tie. Proposition Bets can help players reduce this disadvantage by allowing them to alter their playing strategy as the game progresses.

A DOUBLE DOWN BET lets you increase your initial wager when you only want to take one more hit. Though you can add a smaller sum, you should double your wager.

First, lay your original two cards on the table as though they had been dealt face up. Then place your Double Down wager next to your original wager (never on top of it). The dealer completes the hand by placing a single card underneath the wager.

Typically you can Double Down on any total but only on the original two cards dealt. Some casinos may limit a Double Down wager to certain totals but permit its use even after you have already taken one or more hits. In that instance, a Double Down is generally allowed only on totals of 11, 10, and sometimes 9.

DOUBLE DOWN

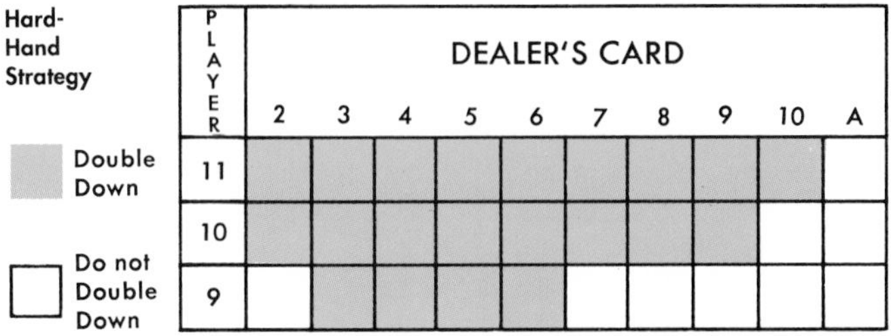

Hard-Hand Strategy

Double Down (shaded)

Do not Double Down (blank)

PLAYER	DEALER'S CARD 2	3	4	5	6	7	8	9	10	A
11	Double Down	Double Down	Double Down	Double Down	Double Down	Double Down	Double Down	Double Down	Double Down	
10	Double Down	Double Down	Double Down	Double Down	Double Down	Double Down	Double Down	Double Down		
9		Double Down	Double Down	Double Down	Double Down					

DOUBLING DOWN WITH A HARD 11 always makes sense because of the possibility of obtaining a Pat hand with no chance of breaking. You should always Double Down with a Hard 10 except when the dealer's face-up card is a 10 or an Ace. Double Down with Hard 10 only when the dealer's face-up card is less than your total of 10 because the dealer can take any number of hits to obtain a Pat hand. Double Down with 9 only when the dealer has a face-up card of 3 to 6. The probability of obtaining a Pat hand is reduced with a Hard 9, so you should double your wager only when the dealer must hit.

DOUBLING DOWN WITH SOFT HANDS of 13 to 18 points is usually advisable whenever the dealer has a face-up card of 4, 5, or 6. This is because of the high probability of the dealer breaking. The diagram below also shows two additional Soft hand situations in which you should always Double Down.

Soft-Hand Strategy

Double Down (shaded)

Do not Double Down (blank)

PLAYER	DEALER'S CARD 2	3	4	5	6	7	8	9	10	A
A-7		Double Down	Double Down	Double Down	Double Down					
A-6		Double Down	Double Down	Double Down	Double Down					
A-5			Double Down	Double Down	Double Down					
A-4			Double Down	Double Down	Double Down					
A-3				Double Down	Double Down					
A-2					Double Down					

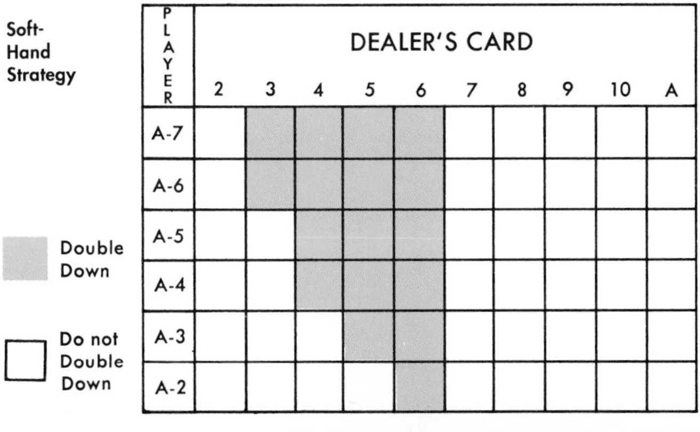

PAIR SPLITTING is allowed when you are dealt two cards of equal value. Most casinos will permit you to split the pair into two independent hands. You first turn the pair face up and separate the two cards, then tuck one of these under the original wager. Lay the other card next to that. An equal wager must then be placed on the second card. You then play out both hands, beginning with the card to the right. The right hand must be completed first, because you cannot return to it after having drawn to the left card. Hit choices are indicated with the hand signals that are used for face-up cards.

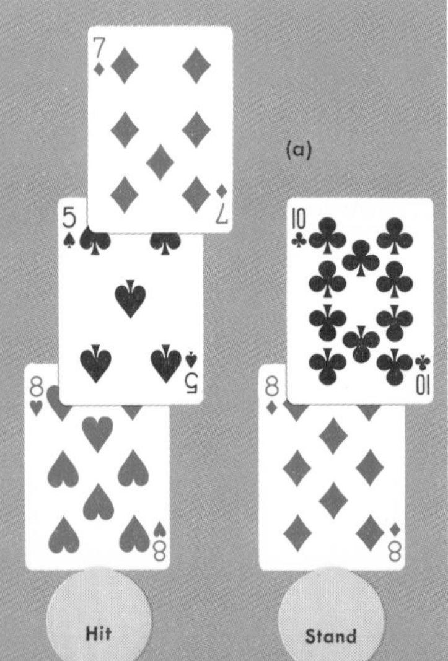

FOR COMPLETING A SPLIT PAIR, several options are available. Once you have drawn to a card from the original pair and produced a new hand of two cards:

a) You may hit or stand.

b) Some casinos also permit you to Double Down, according to established rules.

c) If the first card drawn to either hand produces another pair, you are permitted to split the pair again in many casinos.

d) Casinos usually allow up to four hands to be created from the original pair. (There are twelve face cards in a single deck and at least sixteen of every value card in a four-deck shoe.)

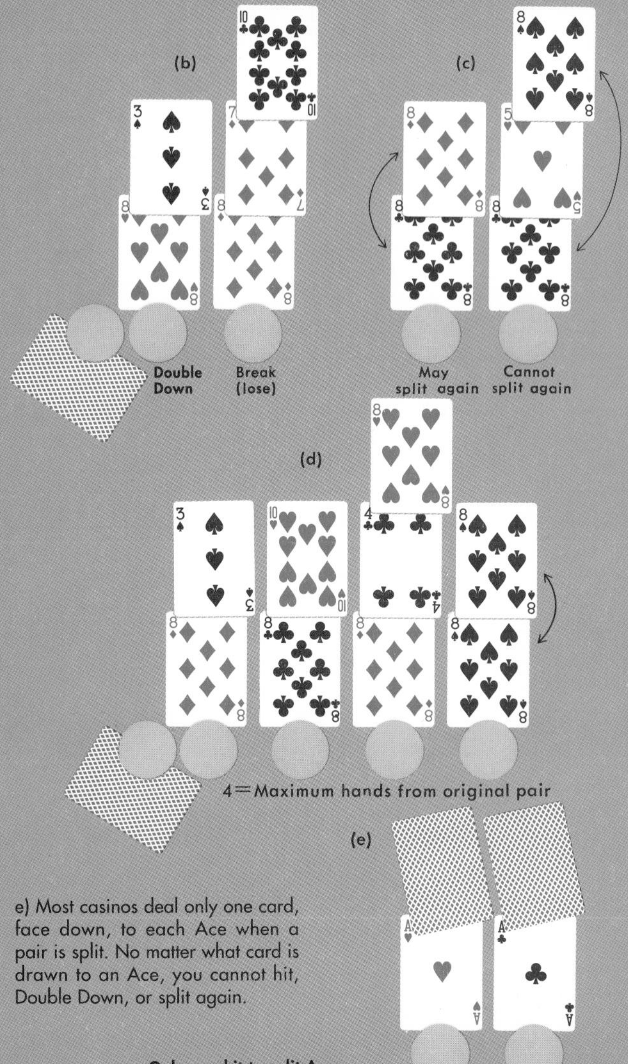

e) Most casinos deal only one card, face down, to each Ace when a pair is split. No matter what card is drawn to an Ace, you cannot hit, Double Down, or split again.

Only one hit to split Aces

PLAYER	DEALER'S CARD 2	3	4	5	6	7	8	9	10	A
A-A	Split	Split	Split	Split	Split	Split	Split	Split	Split	Split
10-10	Do not split	Do not split	Do not split	Do not split	Do not split	Do not split	Do not split	Do not split	Do not split	Do not split
9-9	Split	Split	Split	Split	Split	Do not split	Split	Split	Do not split	Do not split
8-8	Split	Split	Split	Split	Split	Split	Split	Split	Split	Split
7-7	Split	Split	Split	Split	Split	Split	Do not split	Do not split	Do not split	Do not split
6-6	Split	Split	Split	Split	Split	Do not split	Do not split	Do not split	Do not split	Do not split
5-5	Do not split	Do not split	Do not split	Do not split	Do not split	Do not split	Do not split	Do not split	Do not split	Do not split
4-4	Do not split	Do not split	Do not split	Split	Split	Do not split	Do not split	Do not split	Do not split	Do not split
3-3	Split	Split	Split	Split	Split	Split	Do not split	Do not split	Do not split	Do not split
2-2	Split	Split	Split	Split	Split	Split	Do not split	Do not split	Do not split	Do not split

Split pair

Do not split pair

PAIR-SPLITTING STRATEGY is not especially complicated. Always split Aces, even though casinos usually permit only one card to each Ace. Though an Ace and a 10-point card equal 21, after a split they are not treated as Blackjack. But they do pay 1 to 1 except when the dealer also obtains 21 to tie.

A pair of 8's should also be split. Hitting to two hands of 8 is not particularly good, but it is better than one wager on 16. A pair of 10's is never split, because it is better to stand on a total of 20 points. A pair of 5's is also never split because it is better to hit or Double Down on 10 points. It is better to hit one hand of 8 points than to split 4's, except when the dealer's hand shows a 5 or a 6. The rest of the pairs—2's, 3's, 6's, 7's, and 9's—are split only when the dealer has a low face-up card.

INSURANCE is offered by most casinos when the dealer's face-up card is an Ace. After the initial two cards are dealt to each player but before any cards are drawn, the dealer asks, "Insurance?" The players can make an Insurance wager at this time. This wager—a maximum of half the amount of the original wager—is placed directly in front of the player in the Insurance Bet area. Then the dealer looks at the Hole card, and if he or she does not have Blackjack, the Insurance Bet is lost and play continues. However, when the dealer has a 10-point card in the Hole to produce Blackjack, the Insurance Bet wins and the player is paid 2 to 1 (the amount of the original wager).

In some casinos, the dealer's Hole card is not shown until after all player hands are finished. If the dealer has Blackjack, he or she takes the original wagers but returns the Double Down and Split Pair wagers to the players.

THE DECISION TO TAKE INSURANCE, contrary to popular belief, should be made completely independent of the two-card total in your hand. The only relevant factor is the probability of the dealer having a 10 in the Hole. Never take Insurance, no matter what your first two cards are, unless you are keeping track of the discards and know that at least one-third of the cards left in the deck are 10-pointers.

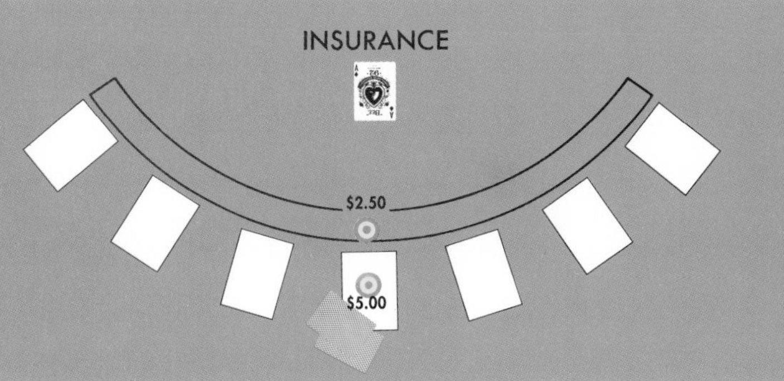

SURRENDERING YOUR HAND BEFORE TAKING A HIT may be allowed. Some casinos permit you to cancel your hand before you draw any cards by surrendering one-half of your wager. It is *very* rare that a hand does not have at least a 25 percent chance of winning, but in that rare case it is better to give the casino one-half of the wager than to face the high risk of losing all of it.

PLAYING MORE THAN ONE HAND

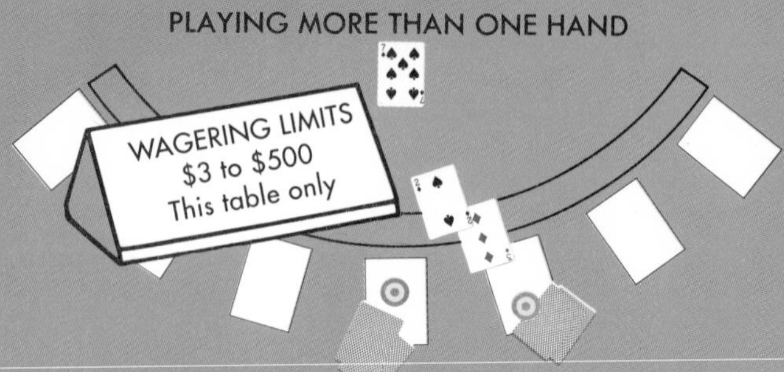

TWO OR MORE HANDS can be wagered on in each deal, but casinos usually require more than the minimum wager for each hand. You may not touch the cards in a hand until you have completed the hand to the right of it except when the dealer has an Ace face up. Then you may look at each hand to decide if you want to take Insurance. It is recommended that beginners not complicate things for themselves by playing more than one hand.

It should be emphasized that the opportunity of winning is the same at every betting location. There is a popular belief among players that "Third Base," the position to the far left of the table, influences what cards the dealer will draw. But strategy decisions at Third Base do not have any overall effect on the dealer's hand.

CARD COUNTING has been shown to be the most effective strategy for playing Blackjack.

When a dealer begins a new hand without shuffling the deck that was used in a previous hand, the composition of the deck is different from the standard 52-card deck that he or she began with. The hand-total probabilities on the next deal are changed. Although the dealer must hit according to fixed rules, players have the flexibility of adjusting their decisions based on the cards that are left in the deck.

By counting the discards after each hand, players can base their playing strategy on what cards remain. They can also increase the amount of their wagers when they see they have a greater chance of winning.

Card counting can indeed be an effective playing strategy. It can reduce the casino advantage to a minimum and actually give players the advantage. There are a lot of books that have been written on this subject, each one with a different counting method and a slightly different calculation of the player's advantage.

Although players can gain the advantage from card counting, they must make a great effort to accurately keep track of all cards, alter their wagers according to the probability of winning in each type of situation, and adjust their playing strategies to situations that are constantly changing. All of this requires a great deal of practice and concentration on the part of the player. In addition, the potential benefits tend to be minimal unless large amounts of money are wagered.

WHEN HIGH CARDS have been discarded from the deck, an excess of low cards remains. Having a greater percentage of low cards increases the probability that the dealer will win the game, because he or she by the rules must hit a Stiff (12 to 16) and can now more easily obtain a Pat hand (17 to 21). In such a situation, low cards work to the dealer's advantage.

The best strategy for players here is to draw according to the dealer's fixed hitting rules and also attempt to obtain a Pat hand. Unfortunately, this strategy increases the possibility of the player's breaking, giving the casino an even greater advantage. In addition, extra-low cards restrict the opportunity to make a Pat hand out of a Double Down, since the player is less likely to draw a high card.

WHEN LOW CARDS have been discarded from the deck, leaving a greater percentage of high cards, the probabilities of the player winning are increased. Blackjacks and high cards for Double Downs become more likely. In the long run, both the dealer and the player will be dealt about the same proportion of low and high cards from the deck. But in those situations where there is a greater percentage of high cards, players using proper hitting strategy can obtain the advantage. Proper hitting strategy means that they should not hit Stiffs (12 to 16) because the probability is too high that they will draw a high card and break. When both the player and dealer have Stiffs, the player should stand and let the dealer hit, hoping the dealer will draw a high card and break.

COUNTING STRATEGIES are beyond the scope of this book, except to explain the principle on which each is based.

ACE COUNTING is a very obvious strategy, because Aces are needed to achieve Blackjack and they make the best pair to split. But it is not the best strategy. As the relative number of Aces to the other cards increases, you can alter your wager but not your playing strategy.

FIVE COUNTING is more effective than Ace counting because you can alter not only the size of your wager but also your playing strategy. For example, the dealer must hit on a Stiff (12 to 16), and 5 points gives him or her a Pat hand (17 to 21). With the 5's discarded, there is a greater probability that the dealer will break.

TEN-POINT COUNTING is even better than five-counting because there are four times as many 10-point cards. Though removing each 10-point card from the deck does not influence the advantage that much, 10-point cards are more important as a group. The 10-count is more accurate and so can help players make subtler strategy moves. Plus, Insurance can be taken whenever it is to the player's advantage (i.e., when there are more than a third of the 10-point cards left in the deck).

NUMBER COUNTING is the most effective strategy there is because it takes into account the influence of every card remaining in the deck. Each card value is given a number equal to its importance in relation to the casino advantage.

As an example, the 2's through 7's might each be given a value of +1 and the 9's, 10's, and Aces given a value of −1. As each card is played from the deck, the +1 or −1 number representing the card is either added to or subtracted from the running total; this depends on whether or not it is to the player's advantage to have it removed from the deck. In this example, each time a low card is dealt, the player would add 1, and each time a high card is dealt, the player would subtract 1.

In using this type of system, the player must either accurately count the number of cards remaining in the deck or estimate their number to determine the casino advantage or disadvantage. Third Base is the best seat for sophisticated counters because they can adjust their hitting strategies after seeing the cards that are dealt to other customers.

A simple plus-minus count, as in the example above, has only one positive number for each low card removed from the deck and the same but negative number for each high card that is removed from the deck. The high-low number count usually makes 8 or else 7, 8, and 9 neutral. They have a minor effect and are thus given a value of 0.

A complex number count assigns a different number to every card. Adding and subtracting is then done as in the other method. This type of counting is the most comprehensive and effective method of analyzing the entire deck to determine the proper size of the wager and the best playing strategy.

COME
HARDWAYS
9 to 1
7 to 1
Double
12

CRAPS

Craps provides faster and more exciting action than any of the other casino games. There are few players who are familiar with all the rules and practices of the game, and even fewer who know the true odds for each betting option. There is no way to win at Craps in the long run, but one can learn more about the game and reduce the rate of loss.

A Crap layout usually has three sections. The two outside sections are identical, so it does not matter at which end of the table a person plays. All players at the table may wager on the Proposition Bets in the center of the layout. A Crap table usually operates with four employees: the Boxman, two dealers, and the Stickman.

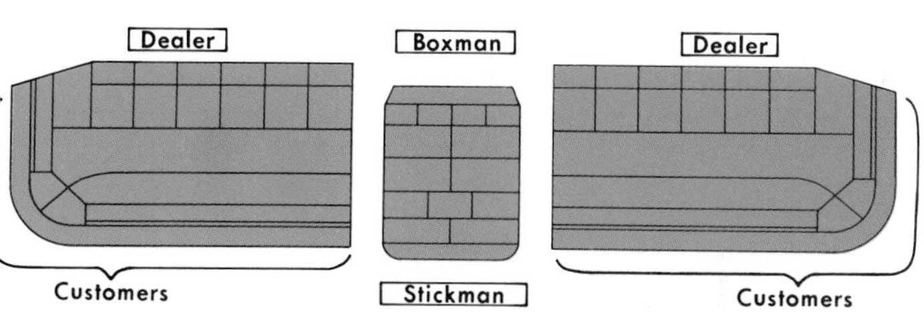

THE BOXMAN sits at the center of the layout; drops all currency into the money box; directs the game; and watches the dice, chips, money, dealers, players, transactions, etc.

THE STICKMAN stands in the center on the players' side of the table and is responsible for handling the dice and the Proposition Bets.

TWO DEALERS stand one on each side of the Boxman and either pay off or collect the wagers on their side of the table. Dealers also make change for the players.

NOTE: In this section on Craps, numbers that represent dice totals are printed in red. This helps to distinguish them from other numbers, which appear in black.

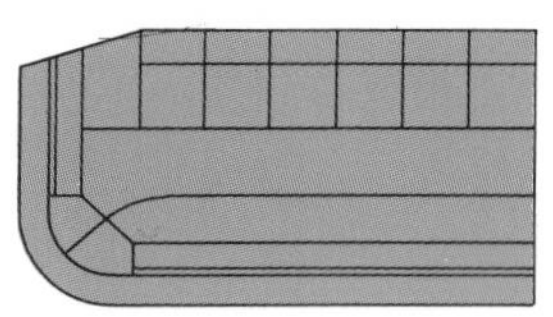

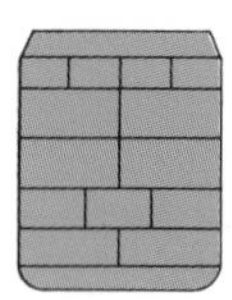

PLAYERS CAN OBTAIN CHANGE by placing currency in front of the dealer and calling out, "Change!" The dealer will usually repeat this, particularly if wagers must be handled first. The dealer then gives the money to the Boxman, who counts it and tells the dealer the amount. Then the dealer places an equivalent amount in chips on the layout directly in front of the player.

Chips should never be left anywhere on the table surface except in the betting areas, because they can get in the way of the dice and they may also be mistaken for wagers. Players should place all extra chips in the special grooves in the top of the table railing directly in front of them.

A player who amasses a lot of chips can have them exchanged for larger-denomination chips so that there will be fewer to carry around. Since each chip denomination is a different color, the player requests a "color change" when the chips are handed in.

It is important to remember that dealers are required to pay off all winning wagers from the previous roll of the dice and set up wagers for players who already have chips before they make change.

PASS LINE BET

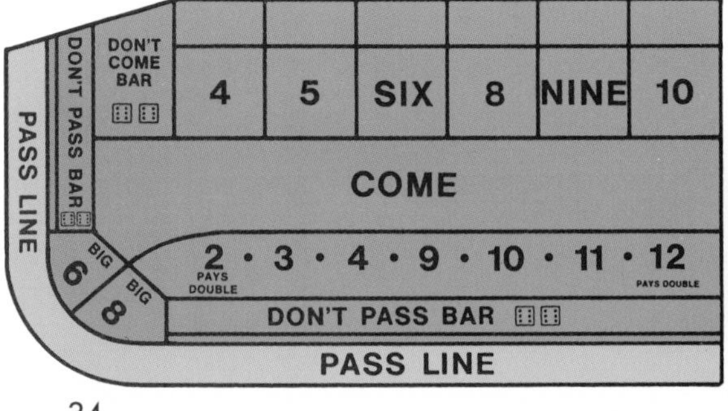

PASS BET RULES

Come-out Roll	Point Rolls
Natural 7 or 11 – WIN	Point – WIN
Crap 2, 3 or 12 – LOSE	7 – LOSE

POINTS

4	5	6	8	9	10

THE PASS LINE BET is the most popular bet in Craps, even though the Don't Pass Bet, which will be explained in detail later on, offers the player a lower casino advantage.

THE FIRST ROLL of the dice for the Pass Line is called the "Come-out roll." On the Come-out, the player wins if a Natural 7 or 11 appears and loses if a Crap 2, 3, or 12 appears. If one of the remaining six totals—4, 5, 6, 8, 9, or 10—appears, it becomes the Pass Line Point. When a Point is rolled on a Come-out, the dealers place a round Point marker directly in front of them in the corresponding numbered Point box.

ON THE POINT ROLL, there are different rules that determine whether the Pass Line Bet will win or lose. The bet will win only if that Point (indicated by the Point marker) appears again, and it will lose only if a 7 appears. The game continues until either the Point or a 7 appears. No other number counts. A Pass Line Bet win pays off at a 1 to 1 ratio. The dealer places an equal amount in chips next to the player's winning wager.

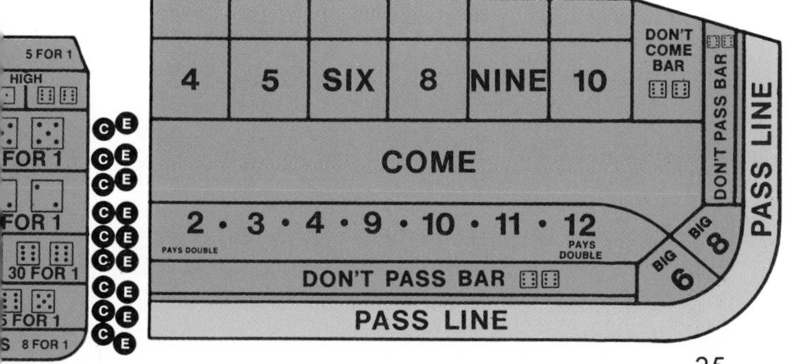

COME-OUT ROLL VS. POINT ROLL

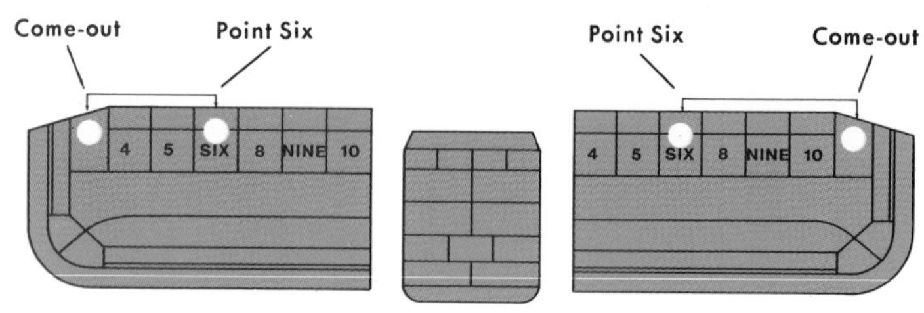

THE COME-OUT ROLL is the first roll of the dice by the first player to make a wager at an empty table. The rules for Come-out rolls are also applied to every roll that follows a winning or losing decision on the Pass Line. For example, when a Come-out roll wins (Natural 7 or 11) or loses (Crap 2, 3, or 12), the next roll is another Come-out. Similarly, when a Point roll wins (a Point appears) or loses (7 appears), the next roll is a Come-out.

At an empty table, or after a decision on the Pass Line of a table in play, the dealers set aside the Point markers on both sides of the layout. They generally place the Point markers in the Don't Come betting box or to the side of the layout but never in any of the six Point boxes. Dealers do not place their markers in a Point box until one of the six Point numbers—for example, a 6—appears on a Come-out roll to become the Point. Dealers do not move their markers back to the Come-out location until the Point appears (in this particular example, a 6) and the player wins, or until a 7 appears and the player loses. A new Come-out roll is then in order.

CUSTOMER'S ADVANTAGE ON COME-OUT ROLL						
In each series of 36 rolls 24 are Points						
Naturals				**Craps**		
Dice Total		**Number of Rolls**		**Dice Total**		**Number of Rolls**
				2	=	1
7	=	6		3	=	2
11	=	2		12	=	1
		WIN 8	— Customer —			LOSE 4

The Come-out roll offers the player the advantage over the casino because there will be an average of 8 Naturals to every 4 Craps. There will be an average of 12 decisions (wins and losses) out of every 36 Come-out rolls. The other 24 rolls will be Points. However, the casino more than compensates for the player's initial advantage once a Point has been established because the casino wins on 7, which appears more often than any other dice total. Once a Point is established, a player cannot remove the Pass Line wager unless he or she wins. If players were allowed to do this, they would be able to retain their initial advantage over the casino and wager only on Come-out rolls.

All bets except the Pass Line with a Point established and Come-out Bets that have moved onto a number can be removed by players at any time. Players have the right to wager on the Pass Line on any roll, but it is advisable never to make or increase a Pass Line wager on a Point roll because of the likelihood of a 7 appearing, giving the casino a big advantage after a Point has been established. Pass Line wagers should be made only on Come-out rolls.

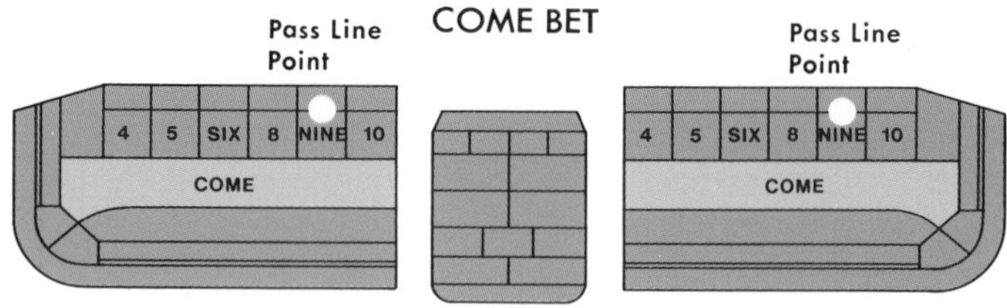

THE COME BET wins and loses according to the Pass Line Bet rules (see page 35). The Pass Line Bet should be made only on Come-out rolls and the Come Bet only when a Point has been established on the Pass Line (when the Point marker is in one of the Point boxes). The player may make a Come wager on every Point roll. A Come wager wins on the next roll if a Natural 7 or 11 appears and loses if a Crap 2, 3, or 12 appears.

When a Come point 4, 5, 6, 8, 9, or 10 appears, the dealer moves the player's wager to that Point box—for example, 4. A Come wager in a Point box wins if that Point number appears (in this example, a 4) and loses if 7 appears. A Come wager cannot be removed from a Point box until it either wins or loses. All wagers at the Crap table, except the Pass Line with a Point established and Come wagers (which have moved onto a number), can be removed by the player at any time. When a Point has been established and a 7 appears,

COME POINT

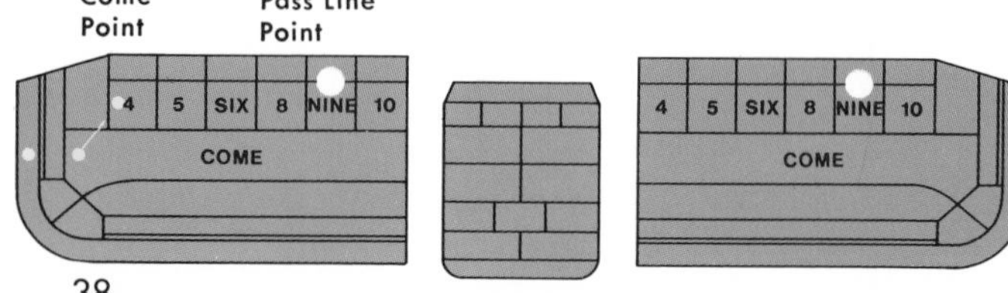

COME PAYOFF

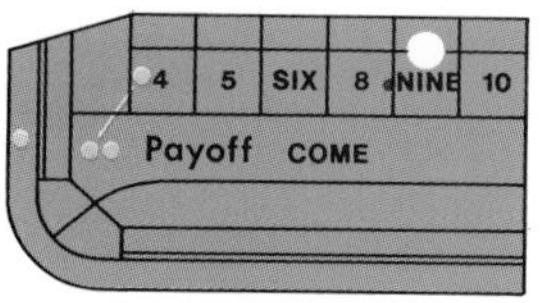

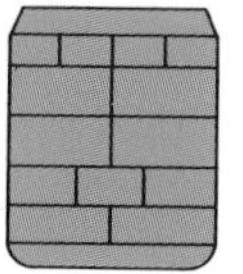
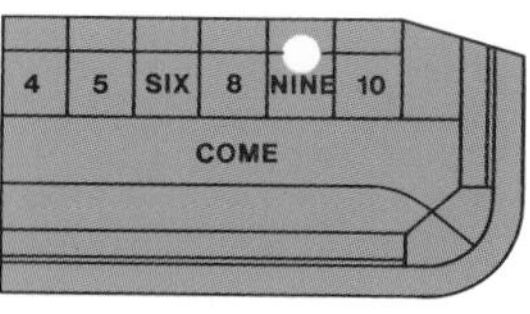

the Pass Line Bet and all Come wagers that have moved onto a Point number lose, but a new wager in the Come Bet wins because for the new bet it is a Come-out roll (and, just like the Pass Line on a Come-out roll, it wins on a 7 or 11 and loses on a 2, 3, or 12).

PAYOFFS FOR WINNING COME BETS on the first roll are placed by the dealer next to the player's wager. When a Come Bet is in a Point box and wins because that Point total appears, the dealer moves the player's wager back to the Come Bet and puts the payoff chips next to it. The Come Bet always pays 1 to 1. The player's wager and the payoff become the wager on the next roll unless the player alters the amount.

THE PLAYER'S POSITION at the table dictates where his or her wager will be placed in the Point box; that way there is no question about who made the wager.

CUSTOMER POINT BOX LOCATION

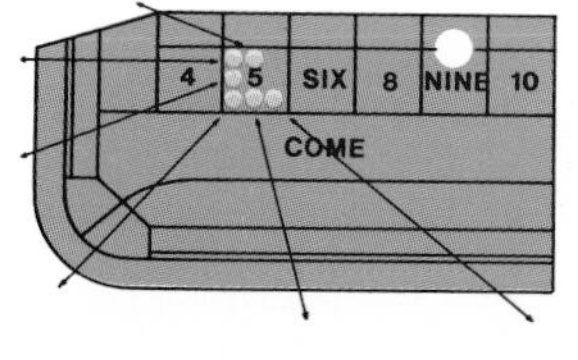

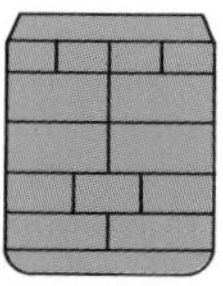
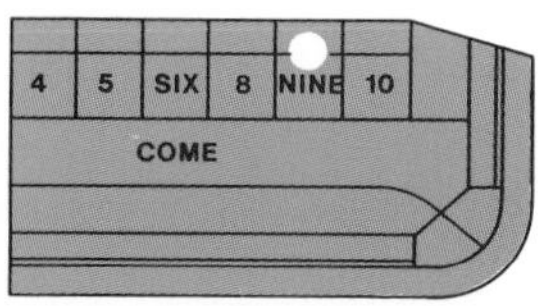

DON'T PASS BET

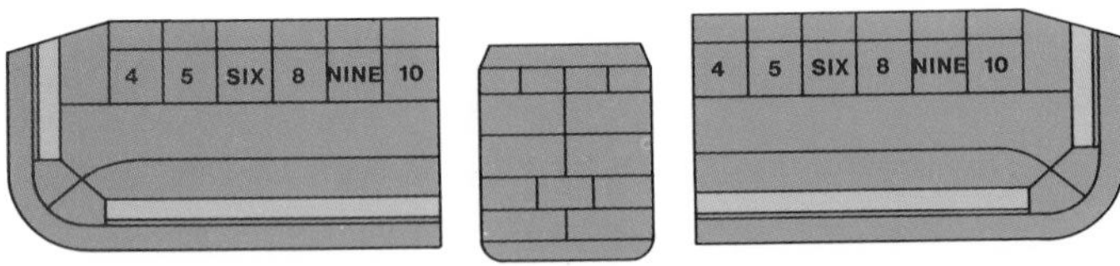

DON'T PASS AND DON'T COME BETS have the lowest casino advantage of all Crap bets. However, the Pass Line and Come bets are much more popular, mainly because of tradition and a general lack of knowledge. These bets lose at an average rate of 12¢ more for each $1,000 wagered than the Don't Pass and Don't Come Bets. The Don't Pass Bet is basically the opposite of the Pass Line Bet. When one wins, the other usually loses, with one important difference (see below).

ON THE COME-OUT ROLL players lose on Natural 7 or 11 and win on Crap 2 or 3 but not on Crap 12. In the Don't Pass and Don't Come betting boxes the picture of the dice shows Barred 12. This means that Crap 12 is a tie (neither wins nor loses), and no money changes hands. After a Barred total appears, players may change their bets or remove them completely.

THE DON'T PASS BET is not the exact opposite of the Pass Line Bet. If it were, players would have the advantage. When Crap 12, which appears on an average of once in every 36 rolls, is Barred, it changes the Don't Pass Bet from a win to a tie. This small difference is enough to give the casino almost the same advantage on both the Pass Line and Don't Pass bets.

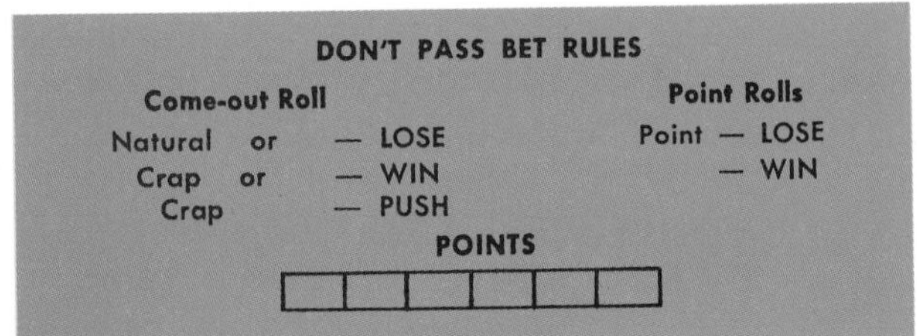

DON'T PASS BET CASINO ADVANTAGE

COME-OUT ROLL

Naturals

Dice Total	=	Number of Rolls
7	=	6
11		2
		LOSE 8

— Customer —

Craps

Dice Total	=	Number of Rolls
2	=	1
3		2
		WIN 3

POINT ROLLS

WIN Dice Total	Number of Rolls	LOSE Dice Totals	Customer Advantage
7 =	6 to 3 =	4 or 10	33.3%
	6 to 4 =	5 or 9	20.0%
	6 to 5 =	6 or 8	9.1%

A DON'T PASS WAGER on a Come-out roll gives the casino a large advantage over the player. In every 36 Come-outs, the player will win an average of only 3 wagers while losing 8. However, once a point is established, the casino advantage is reduced because the player wins on 7, which appears more often than the other numbers. A player with a Point on the Don't Pass has a large advantage over the casino. Don't Pass and Don't Come are the only bets that you cannot make or add to once a Point has been established, because you have the advantage. However, the casino will permit you to remove your Don't Pass wager at any time, because then you are giving up your strong advantage. Obviously, you should never do this. Note that the Pass Line and Come Bet rules are just the opposite. They permit the player to make a wager at any time but prohibit him or her from removing the wager once a Point has been established.

These are the only restrictions on adding and removing wagers. Every other bet allows the player the option of adding to the original wager or removing it on every roll of the dice.

DON'T BET—BARRED NUMBERS

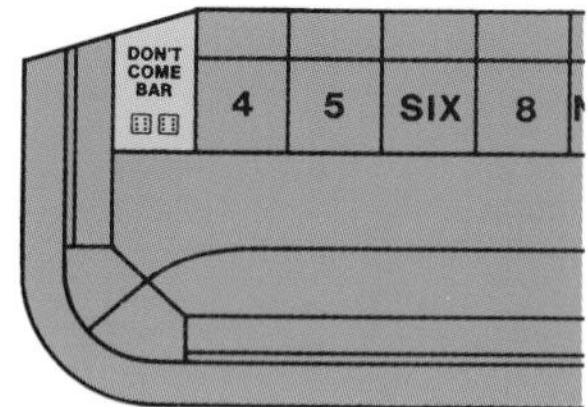

4
5
SIX
8
NINE
DON'T PASS
DON'T COME

IN MOST AREAS, the Don't Come Bet is located in the rear corners of the layout. Players should stand near these when making Don't Come wagers so they don't have to reach a long distance to place the wager and retrieve the winnings.

IN NORTHERN NEVADA, the Don't Come runs parallel to the Pass Line around the entire layout. There is no Don't Pass on these layouts; a player who wants to wager on the Don't Pass must put it on the Don't Come Bet.

CRAP 12 IS BARRED on the Don't wagers in most locations. In a few casinos, mostly in northern Nevada, Crap 2 is Barred. Since Crap 2 and 12 have the same probability of occurring—1 in every 36 rolls—this change does not really affect the casino advantage. However, it does affect the specific numbers on which the player wins and pushes (ties). As the game has matured and players have become more sophisticated, the practice of Barring Crap 3 (which doubles the casino advantage) has almost disappeared. Any Don't wager is a relatively bad choice with a Barred Crap 3.

The Don't Come Bet has the same win, lose, and Barred rules as the Don't Pass, and except for the Barred number, it has the opposite rules of the Come Bet. The player may make a Don't Come wager on each and every Point roll.

DON'T COME POINT BET

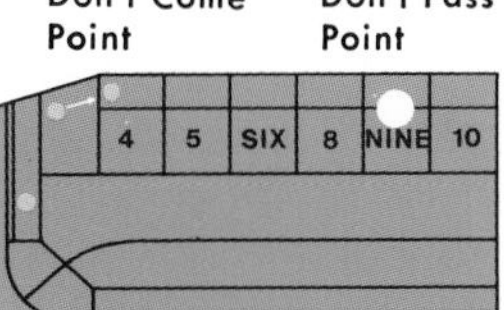

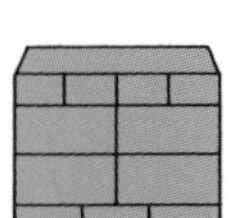
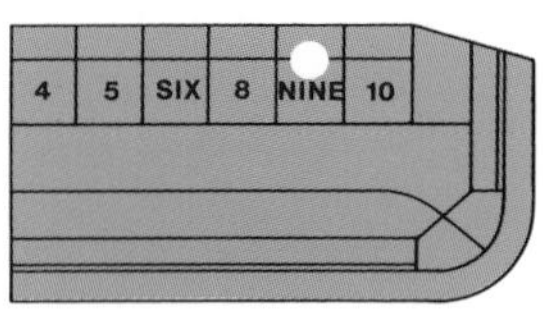

WHENEVER A POINT—4, 5, 6, 8, 9, or 10—appears, the dealer moves the wager to the box above that Point number. A Don't Come wager wins if Crap 2 or 3 appears, loses if Natural 7 or 11 appears, and ties if Barred 12 appears. The Don't Come Point boxes do not have any numbers showing, but players should imagine a 7 in each because they win when 7 appears and lose if the Point number contained in the box below it appears, in this example, a 4. When a player has several Don't Come wagers in the Don't Come Point boxes, he or she loses only one at a time as the respective Points appear, but wins them all at once when a 7 appears. However, when a 7 does appear, the player loses the wager in the Don't Come Bet because it is treated according to the same rules as those for Come-out rolls.

PAYOFFS FOR DON'T COME BETS are placed next to the player's wager when a Don't Come Bet wins on the first roll. When a Don't Come wager is in a Don't Come Point box, it wins when a 7 appears. The dealer places the payoff chips next to the winning wager before moving the wager and the payoff back to the Don't Come box. When the player has wagers in more than one Don't Come Point box, the dealer pays them off in the boxes and piles the entire amount in the Don't Come box. The Don't Come Bet always pays off at 1 to 1. All of the chips remain in the Don't Come box as the wager for the next roll unless the player changes the amount.

DON'T COME PAYOFF

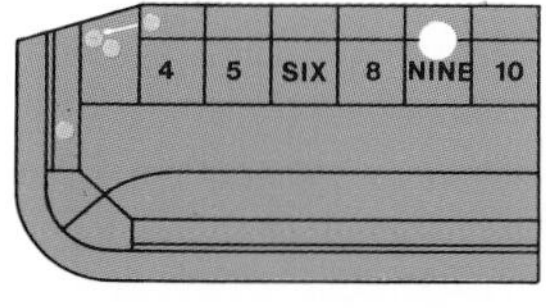

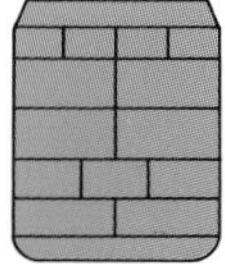
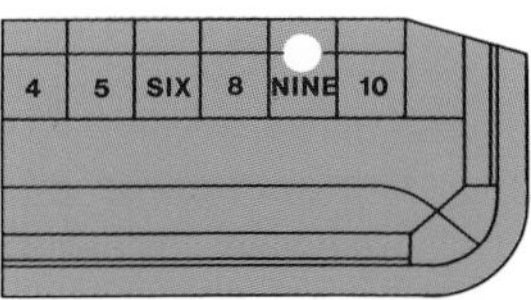

THE STICKMAN controls the dice, which are kept in a bowl nearby.

Usually there are five dice offered to a player. The player selects any two of these and immediately picks them up and throws them. The dice should be thrown past the Stickman, and should be thrown firmly enough to make them bounce off the other end of the table.

After each roll, the Stickman announces the total, pulls in the dice with a long stick, and places them in the center of the table in front of the Boxman. When the dealers have collected and paid off all of the wagers, the Stickman sends the dice back to the player, who immediately picks them up and shoots them again.

A player must wager on either the Pass Line or on the Don't Pass when shooting the dice and can make any additional wagers at any time. Other players can also wager on any bet or on any combination of bets they desire.

The shooter loses the dice only on a throw of 7 on a Point roll but can elect to pass the dice to the next player at any time. The dice cannot be lost on a Come-out roll, and they can be lost on a Point roll only when a 7 appears. When a player is finished shooting, the Stickman, moving in a clockwise fashion, offers all of the dice in the bowl to the next player.

The player who has the dice should always keep them in view of the Stickman. If at any time they are concealed, the Stickman will ask for them to be examined by the Boxman and will offer the player another pair of dice from the bowl. Any player who continues to remove the dice from view will then be prohibited from shooting.

If a player does not want to shoot the dice, he or she makes a waving motion toward the left. The Stickman then offers the dice to the next player.

Players shooting dice at the Grand Casino in Mississippi

THE DICE are considered out of play and the roll nullified if one or both of them bounce off the table. The Stickman announces, "No roll!" and offers the remaining dice to the player to select another pair. No money is collected or paid out, and players may change their wagers. If both of the dice land on the table, the roll is counted unless one ends up in the dice bowl, on the stacks of chips stored in front of the Boxman, or in the metal racks that some casinos have positioned in front of the dealers.

THE ODDS BET is the only bet that does not give the casino an advantage. In the long run, the casino will not come out ahead of the players. Odds is offered by the casino as a courtesy bet to stimulate wagering on the Pass Line, Come, Don't Pass, and Don't Come bets. These four bets have a low casino advantage, and the addition of Odds makes them even more attractive. Because the casino does not expect to profit on the Odds Bet, wagering on it should be the prime objective of the Craps player. Odds can be wagered only on the Point rolls of these four bets. Every time a Point is established, you should add an Odds wager to your Pass Line, Come, Don't Pass, or Don't Come wager.

AN ODDS WAGER may be put behind the player's Pass Line wager when a Point, for example, a 5, is established. Both wagers win when the Point appears, in this example, a 5, and both wagers lose when a 7 appears. When the wagers win, the Pass Line wager is paid off 1 to 1, but the Odds wager is paid off by the ratio of the probability of 7 to the probability of the Point. In this example, 5 is paid off 3 to 2. After winning, the Odds wager must be removed because it can be taken only on Point rolls, and the next roll is a Come-out. Pass Line, Come, Don't Pass, and Don't Come wagers are called "Flat" wagers because the payoff is 1 to 1. The stack of chips for the payoff is the same height as the wager; thus, the wager is paid off "Flat." This terminology distinguishes a Flat and an Odds wager on the same bet because Odds wagers are always paid off at a ratio of more than 1 to 1.

ODDS BET ON PASS LINE

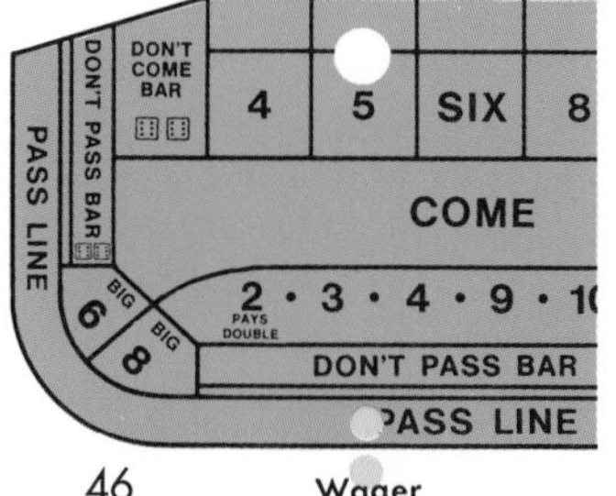

Wager

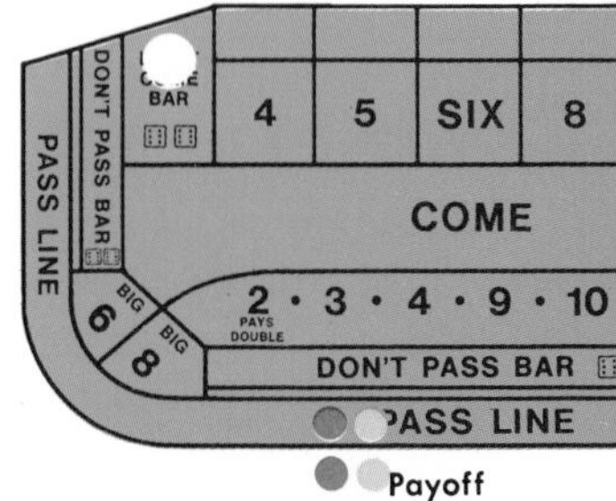

Payoff

ODDS BET ON COME

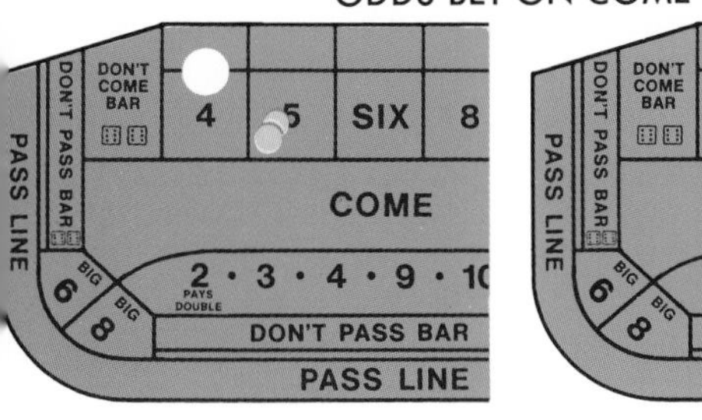

Wager

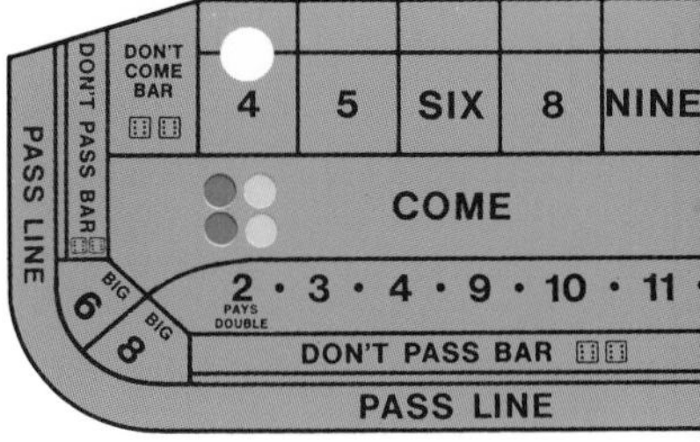

Payoff

ODDS ON A COME WAGER may be made when the Come wager has been moved to a Point box. The player puts the Odds wager on the Come and identifies the Point to the dealer, for example, "Odds on 5." Because the two wagers receive different payoffs, the dealer sets the Odds wager on top of, but slightly ahead of, the player's Come wager. If a 7 appears, both wagers lose. If the Point appears—in this example, a 5—both wagers win. The dealer moves both wagers back to the Come Bet and pays them off. The Come wager is paid 1 to 1, and the Odds wager is paid off by the ratio of the probability of 7 to the probability of the Point. In this example, the Point 5 pays 3 to 2. All of the chips (the two wagers and the two payoffs) remain on the Come for the next roll unless the player removes all or some of them.

Players must take care that the dealer has placed the Odds wagers properly on the Come wagers. If a player always wagers the correct amount on Odds after each point has been rolled, the dealer will come to expect the wager, and no further conversation between the two is necessary.

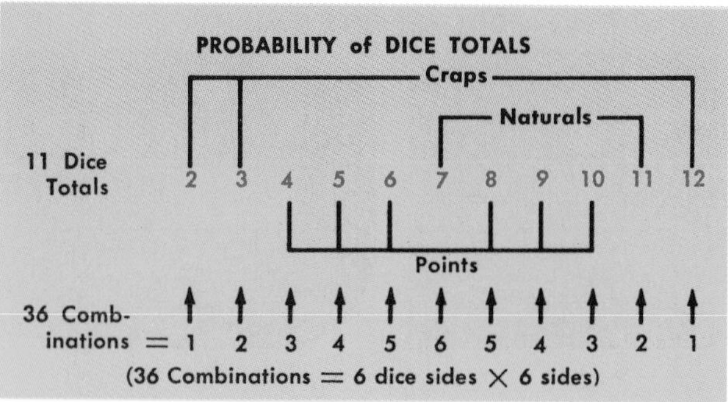

THE PROBABILITY RATIO of the appearance of a 7 to that of each of the six Points—4, 5, 6, 8, 9, or 10—is the basis for the Odds Bet. A pair of dice produces thirty-six different combinations (6 sides x 6 sides = 36 combinations) but only eleven dice totals, 2 through 12. These eleven totals do not share the same probability of appearing. For example, a 7 appears six times while 2 and 12 each appear only once. Odds Bets are created when two of these probabilities are combined into a ratio. A 7 is produced by six combinations of the dice, but the Points are produced by only three, four, or five combinations. Therefore, a player who has a Pass Line or a Come wager with a Point established loses more often than wins because a 7 appears more often than any of the Points.

When the Point does appear, the Flat wager is paid 1 to 1, but the Odds wager is paid 6 to 3 for Points 4 and 10, 6 to 4 for Points 5 and 9, and 6 to 5 for Points 6 and 8. These payoff ratios are based on the probability of a 7 appearing compared to the probability of each of the respective Points appearing.

ODDS PAYOFF RATIOS

Total		Payoff		Totals
7	=	6 to 3	=	4 or 10
7	=	6 to 4	=	5 or 9
7	=	6 to 5	=	6 or 8

THE ODDS PAYOFFS equal the probability of the Point losing to a 7. For example, a 7 is produced by six different combinations, but Point 4 is produced by only three different ones in each series of thirty-six rolls. With Point 4, the Odds Bet will lose an average of six times for every three times it wins. But when 4 appears, the Odds Bet is paid off 6 to 3. This payoff compensates the player for the greater number of losses with Point 4. The casino and players break even in the long run; there is no casino advantage.

SINGLE ODDS refers to the fact that the player cannot wager more on Odds than the amount of the Flat wager. Odds Bets, which have no casino advantage, are offered to stimulate wagering on the Pass Line, Come, Don't Pass, and Don't Come bets. Casinos do not make any profit on Odds Bets, so they restrict the size of Odds wagers in proportion to that of the Flat wager.

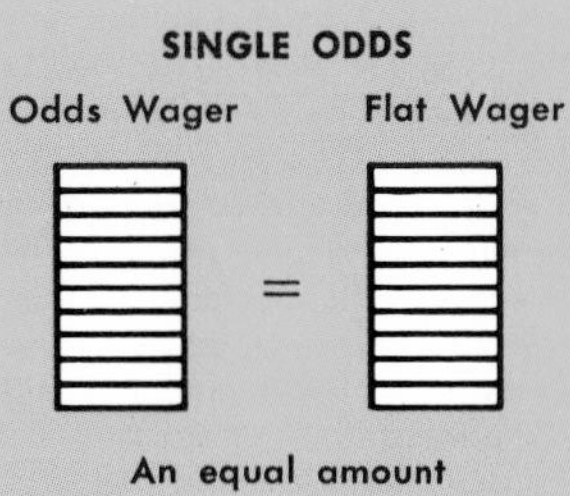

WAGERS LARGER THAN SINGLE ODDS are permitted by most casinos. Since the casino has no advantage on the Odds Bet, players should wager the maximum odds allowed, even if a limited bankroll requires them to reduce the size of their Flat wagers on which the casino has the advantage. Players should ask what is the maximum ratio of the Odds wager to the Flat wager allowed.

FULL ODDS, offered by most casinos, let the player wager a greater amount than Single Odds on Points 5, 6, 8, and 9 in those situations when the correct payoff can't be made for Single Odds. The Point 5 pays 3 to 2, so an Odds wager in an odd amount of dollars would require 50¢ for the payoff (e.g., $5 pays $7.50). However, Crap tables never have coins even though they always have $1 chips for payoffs. Full Odds means the player may add another chip to the Odds wager to make it an even dollar amount—in this case making it $6 so it can be paid in the true odds of 3 to 2 ($9 to $6 here), as explained in detail on the next page. Since the Points 4 and 10 each pay 2 to 1, any wager made in multiples of the table minimum may be paid off correctly, 2 to 1, so Single Odds remains in effect.

FULL ODDS

Totals	Payoffs	Amount of Odds Wager
4 or 10	2 to 1	Equals amount of Flat wager
5 or 9	3 to 2	Next even amount of chips
6 or 8	6 to 5	Nearest multiple of 5 chips

A FLAT WAGER that has an odd amount of chips on a Point of 5 or 9 may be remedied by adding one chip to the Odds wager to make it an even amount of chips. If you have a Flat wager of three $5 chips, for a total of $15, you can add a $1 chip to create an even wager of $16, or another chip of the denomination being wagered, say $5, for a total of $20. A chip of the wagered denomination will add more money to the layout with no casino advantage.

The Points 6 and 8 pay 6 to 5. The correct Odds payoff can be made only if the player bets multiples of five chips—i.e., five, ten, fifteen, etc. When the player has a Flat wager of one or two chips over a multiple of five, the previous multiple of five can be wagered. For example, if there is a Flat wager of two chips, the player may not make an Odds wager. If there is a Flat wager of seven chips, the player is two chips over the previous multiple of five—all that can be wagered on the Odds Bet paying 6 to 5.

When the player has a Flat wager of three or four chips over a multiple of five, he or she can wager the next multiple of five. For example, with a Flat wager of three chips, the Odds wager should be five chips. On a Flat wager with eight chips (5 + 3) the player is three chips over the previous multiple of five and so may wager the next multiple of five, with ten chips on the Odds Bet.

Some casinos may offer a few more variations on Single Odds. Inquire at your casino about these opportunities to obtain Odds Bets that are even larger than Flat Bets.

Odds wagers should always be made in multiples for correct payoffs, or the casino will pay 1 to 1 on the short multiples. The 3 to 2 payoff becomes only 2 to 2, and 6 to 5 becomes only 5 to 5 for partial multiples. When you have a short multiple, you may be tempted to add chips to your Flat wager so you can increase the Odds wager to the next payoff multiple. DON'T! A Flat wager has a large disadvantage once a Point has been established. The increased Odds wager, which has no advantage, cannot compensate for this greater disadvantage.

THE MAXIMUM PROPORTION OF ODDS are obtained when the player makes a Flat wager of three chips. The amount of the Odds wager is determined by the amount of the Flat wager. Therefore, the player should make Flat wagers only in amounts that permit him or her to maximize the amount wagered on the Odds Bets. When the player makes a Flat wager of three chips, the Odds wager should also be three chips for Points 4 and 10, four chips for Points 5 and 9, and five chips for Points 6 and 8. The payoff is always six chips for the

Odds wager and three chips for the Flat wager. If the player wagers the table minimum, one chip, he or she should take Odds of one chip on the Points 4 and 10 and two chips on 5 and 9. Odds on 6 and 8 are not allowed because these require a Flat wager of at least three chips.

MAXIMIZING FULL ODDS

Flat Wager = 1 Chip			Flat Wager = 3 Chips		
Odds Wager	**Totals**	**Payoff**	**Odds Wager**	**Totals**	**Payoff**
1 Chip	or	2 to 1	3 Chips	or	6 to 3
2 Chips	or	3 to 2	4 Chips	or	6 to 4
0 Chips	or	0	5 Chips	or	6 to 5

DOUBLE ODDS are now found in most casinos around the country. A few still have "Double the Flat Bet Odds," which means that the player can bet twice as much on the Odds Bet as on the Flat. The vast majority of casinos offer "True Double Odds," which means the player can wager even more because it is calculated in certain cases by doubling the amount that would be allowed with Full Single Odds (see pp. 49–50). That is why this information is so important. It is the basis for calculating True Double Odds. Just as with Full Single Odds, it is best to wager three chips to obtain the maximum proportion of Odds with True Double Odds. With the Points 4 and 10, the Odds wager is exactly double the Flat wager. With the Points 5 and 9, the Odds is also exactly double the Flat except when the Flat wager is three chips and the Odds can be eight chips. This is because three chips Flat with Full Single Odds would be four (double this is eight chips). The benefit really shows with Points 6 and 8, when the accepted Odds to Flat wagers are: five chips Odds with two chips Flat, ten with three chips, and twenty with six chips. Thus, a three-chip Flat wager permits the highest proportion of Odds on Points 5, 6, 8, and 9. Depending on the point, with three chips Flat, the Odds wager would be six chips (Points 4 and 10), eight chips (Points 5 and 9), or ten chips (Points 6 and 8). There is more on True Double Odds on page 57. Some casinos even offer higher multiples (3 to 10 times) on Odds to Flat wagers.

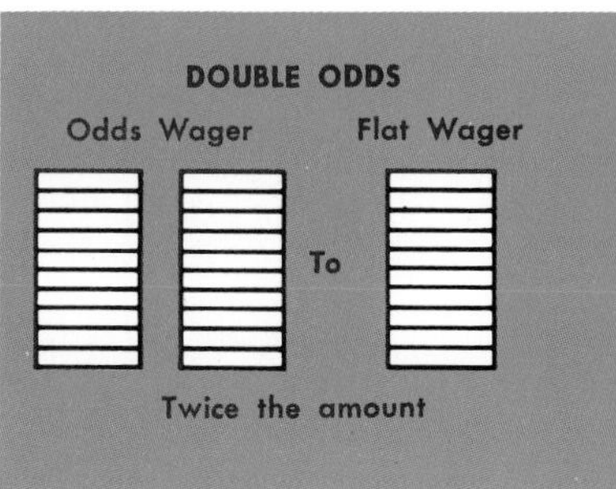

THE ODDS, PLACE, AND BUY WAGERS all lose when 7 appears, but on Come-out rolls the Pass Line wins with the same 7. Most players wager on the Pass Line, so they remove their Odds, Place, and Buy wagers on Come-outs because they do not want to lose them when they win on the Pass Line.

However, removal of these wagers has no statistical effect because the likelihood of getting a 7 remains constant on every roll. It would be a waste of time to remove all these wagers on Come-out rolls and replace them again on Point rolls. Thus the Odds, Place, and Buy wagers are left on the layout on Come-out rolls, but are considered "off," which means that they neither win nor lose. If a Point appears, a Come wager wins and is paid off, but the Odds wager on top of it is returned to the player with no payoff. If a 7 appears, the Come wager loses and is collected, but the Odds wager is returned to the player.

If you want these wagers to count on every roll of the dice, inform the dealer by telling him or her that the wagers "work" on Come-out rolls. The dealer will place either the Point marker or a small "On" button on top of your wager.

BETS "ON" ON COME-OUT ROLL

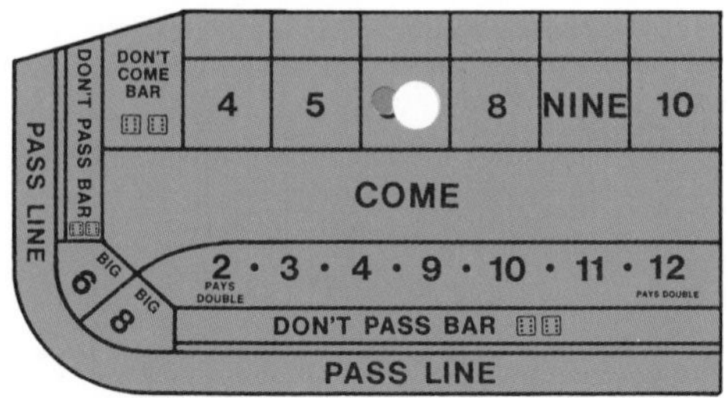

ODDS BET ON DON'T PASS

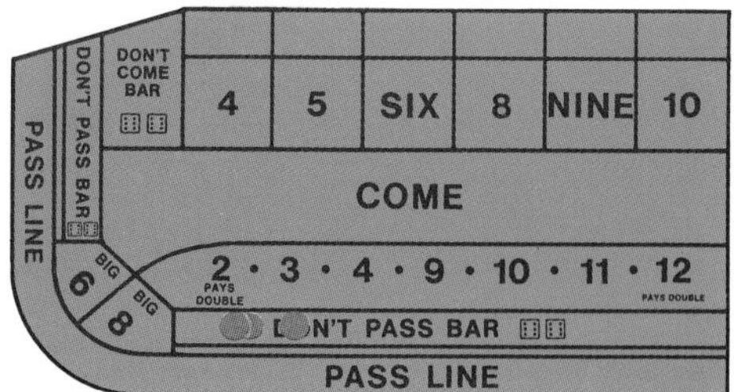

ODDS ON THE DON'T PASS may be laid on Point rolls. The principle here is the same as for the Pass Line, but the terminology is different. On the Pass Line and Come wagers, the player may "take" Odds, and on the Don't Pass and Don't Come, the player may "lay" Odds. The player lays the Odds wager next to the Flat wager by tilting the chips so that they are off the edge of the bottom chip.

ODDS ON A DON'T COME wager can be laid after it has been moved to a Don't Come Point box. The player puts an Odds wager on the Don't Come Bet and identifies the Point, for example, "Lay the 5." The dealer lays the Odds next to the Flat wager. If the Point appears, both wagers lose. If a 7 appears, both wagers win. The dealer moves both of the wagers, along with the payoffs, to the Don't Come Bet. Unlike Odds wagers in Come Point boxes, Odds wagers in Don't Come Point boxes always work, even on Come-out rolls.

ODDS BET ON DON'T COME

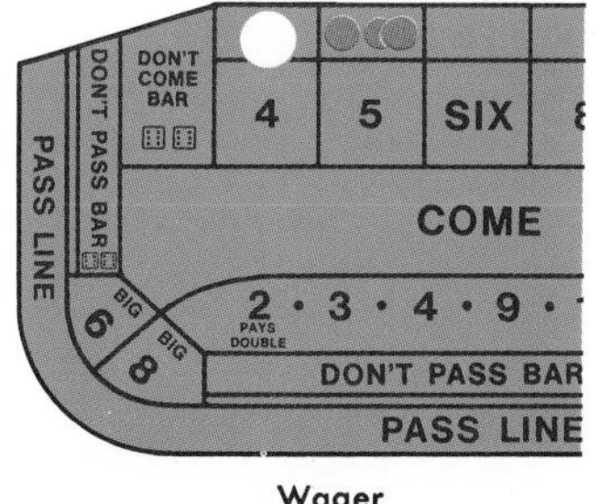

Wager

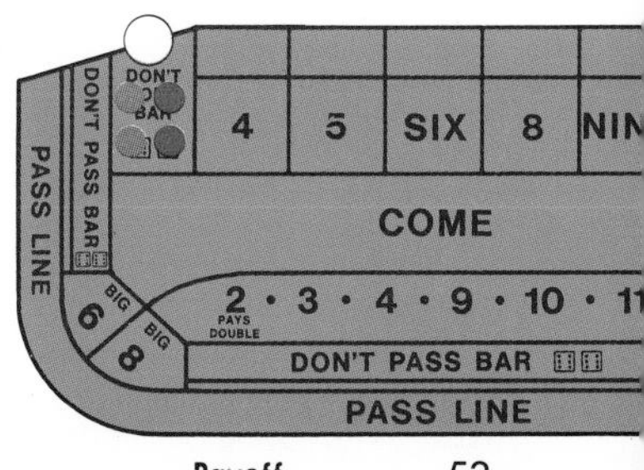

Payoff

PAYOFF RATIOS FOR DON'T BET ODDS	
Totals	**Payoff**
4 or 10	1 to 2
5 or 9	2 to 3
6 or 8	5 to 6

FULL ODDS FOR DON'T PASS BETS have the exact reverse payoff ratios of the Odds Bets on the Do Pass Line. For example, a Pass Line Odds wager on Point 4 is paid off 2 to 1, while a Don't Pass Odds wager on Point 4 is paid off 1 to 2. When one wins, the other loses.

When the player lays the Odds on the Don't Pass, the Odds payoff is always less than the amount of the Odds wager because the player wins more often than loses (7 appears more often than any Point). The player has a greater probability of winning and so is paid less proportionately. The casino and players break even in the long run; there is no casino advantage.

MAXIMIZING FULL ODDS for Don't bets is always desirable. When the Don't Pass and the Pass Line have the same size Flat wager, the amount of the Don't Pass Full Odds wager is the payoff for a Pass Line Full Odds wager. The Don't Pass Full Odds payoff ratios are the reverse of the Do Pass Full Odds ratios (see page 51). The player calculates the amount of the Full Odds wager and its payoff for a Pass Line wager of the same size and then wagers that payoff on Don't Pass Odds. If the player wagers the table minimum, one chip, he or she should lay Odds of two chips on Points 4 and 10 and three chips on 5 and 9. The player cannot lay Odds on 6 and 8 because a Flat wager of at least three units is required. The player obtains the maximum proportions of Odds when making a Flat wager of three chips. The player lays Odds of six chips on all Points and wins three chips for Points 4 and 10, four chips for 5 and 9, and five chips for 6 and 8.

MAXIMIZING FULL ODDS FOR DON'T BETS

Flat Wager = 1 Chip

Odds Wager	Totals	Payoff
2 Chips	4 or 10	1 to 2
3 Chips	5 or 9	2 to 3
0 Chips	6 or 8	0

Flat Wager = 3 Chips

Odds Wager	Totals	Payoff
6 Chips	4 or 10	3 to 6
6 Chips	5 or 9	4 to 6
6 Chips	6 or 8	5 to 6

USING THE "DO" AND "DON'T" BETS WITH FULL ODDS

1) Beginners should make only one bet at a time so as not to be confused by the speed of the game. A good way to start is by making a Pass Line wager and later adding Odds on the Point rolls.

2) More experienced players should also try wagering on the Come bet and learn to take Odds on it. Players who want to get the most action for their money can wager on the Pass Line or Come bet on every roll with Full Odds.

3) The Don't bets should also be learned systematically. Beginners should make only Don't Pass wagers and then lay the Odds. Next, they should make Don't Come wagers and lay the Odds. Eventually, all players acquire the ability and knowledge to wager on any roll desired.

4) Players should make only those Crap bets that have already been discussed in this section—the DO bets (Pass Line and Come), which are the most popular ones on the layout, or the DON'T bets (Don't Pass and Don't Come), which have the lowest casino advantage. In addition, players should always take or lay Double Odds or Full Odds on Point rolls.

5) Players should have a thorough understanding of what they are doing *before* wagering. They should know the amount and location of each wager and where the dealer will move them on the layout, as well as the amount and location of the payoff.

6) Players are fully responsible for their own money. If they have more bets on the table than they can follow, they may not notice a mistake made by the dealer or by other players who may by accident pick up their wager.

7) Players should make themselves clearly understood and ask questions about anything they do not understand. Because a dealer will quickly learn a regular player's patterns and be able to predict his or her next wager, players should be sure to make their intentions known when altering their normal pattern of play.

8) Players must notify the casino immediately if they are unhappy with a situation, because the next roll of the dice will eliminate the grounds of the claim. Such complaints are always taken seriously, and attempts are made to settle them to the player's satisfaction.

The following pages (56–77), which come under the heading **CRAPS IN OPERATION,** illustrate the game as it would actually be played if the dice were thrown in the order shown.

CRAPS IN OPERATION (pages 58–77) consists of a series of Crap table layouts. The left section of each layout contains Do wagers with Full Odds, and the right section contains Don't wagers with Full Odds. The similarities and differences of the Do and Don't wagers can be observed by comparing these sections.

The two center wagers have three chips each. The side wagers have only one chip each. By following one of these wagers through the series of layouts, you can quickly learn the proper ratios for Full Odds.

Color and graphics have been used to identify and differentiate the wagers from the payoffs. Here is what the colors and symbols mean:

➤ Yellow chips represent newly made wagers for the current roll of the dice. Orange chips represent wagers that remain on the table from previous throws of the dice. Red chips represent payoffs made by the dealers.

➤ An "X" mark over a customer's wager signifies that the bet was lost and the dealer collected the wager.

➤ An arrow indicates that a dealer has moved a customer's wager from one position to another.

➤ The number highlighted in the center of each layout is the dice number rolled after the wagers were placed.

➤ A single circle represents a pile of chips. The number beside it equals the number of chips in that pile.

➤ One circle overlapping another is the symbol used for one pile of chips stacked on top of another pile. On left-hand pages, the fraction next to one of these symbols identifies both the number of chips in the Odds

Bet and the number of chips in the Come Bet. For example, the fraction $\frac{5}{3}$ means that five chips for the Odds Bet have been placed on top of but slightly off center of the three chips for the Come Bet. See the diagram at the top of page 58 as an example.

➤ When the symbol of a circle overlapping another circle is used on a right-hand page, it represents an Odds Bet for either a Don't Pass or a Don't Come Bet. In this case, the number next to the symbol represents the Odds Bet only. For instance, the number 6 means that five chips are leaning against a single chip, giving a total of six for the Odds Bet. See the diagram on the right at the top of page 59 for an example.

A newcomer to the game of Craps would do well to study carefully the layouts on the next twenty pages, which show the effects resulting from successive throws of the dice. Since the Odds Bets are the only ones where the player has no disadvantage, they are the most attractive ones on which to make wagers. See pages 46–55 for a detailed explanation of Odds Bets.

NOTE: The following series of layouts is based on the concept of Full Single Odds (see pages 49 and 50). However, most casinos now offer True Double Odds (see page 51). Full Single Odds are presented here because they are the basis for calculating True Double Odds, which are then easier to learn. With one chip wagered on the Do, the True Double Odds wager would always be two chips. Assuming these are $5 chips, the $10 Odds wager would pay $20 for Points 4 and 10, $15 for Points 5 and 9, and $12 for Points 6 and 8. With three $5 chips wagered on the Do, the True Double Odds wagers would be twice as many as for the Full Single Odds presented in the following layouts, meaning six chips or a $30 wager for Points 4 and 10, eight chips or a $40 wager for Points 5 and 9, and ten chips or a $50 wager for Points 6 and 8. The payoff for all these Odds wagers would be $60. For the Don't Odds wagers, the wagers and payoffs for the Do Odds would be reversed, the payoffs becoming the wagers and vice versa. For example, with three $5 chips on the Don't Flat, the Odds wager would always be $60 to win $30, $40, or $50, depending on the Point.

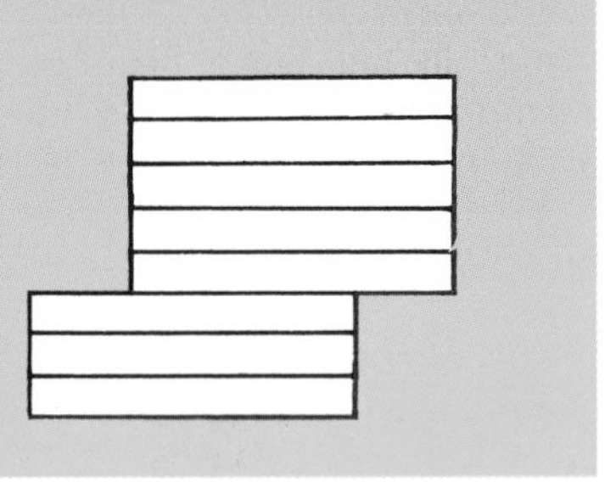

ODDS ON A COME BET

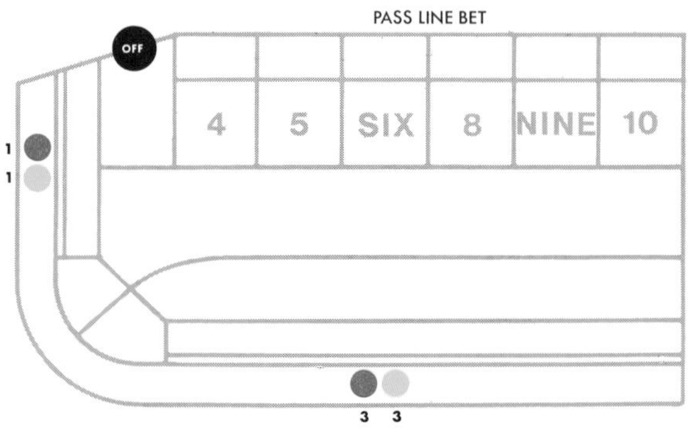

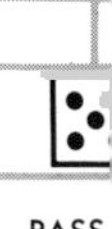

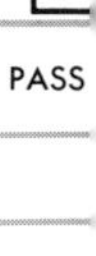

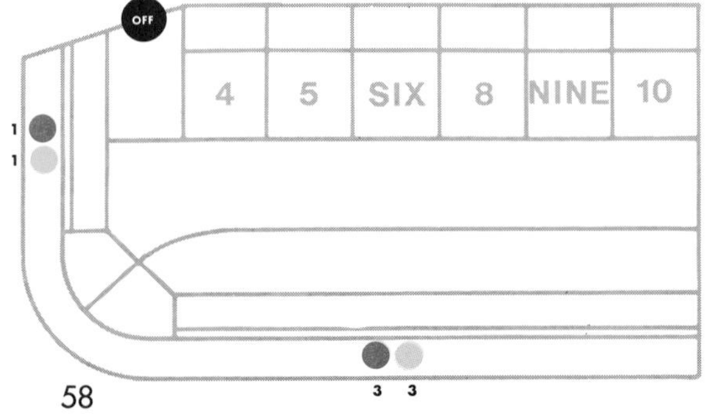

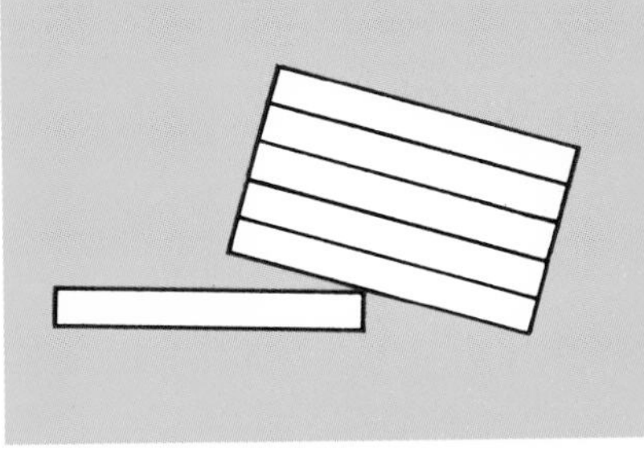

ODDS ON A DON'T COME OR DON'T PASS BET

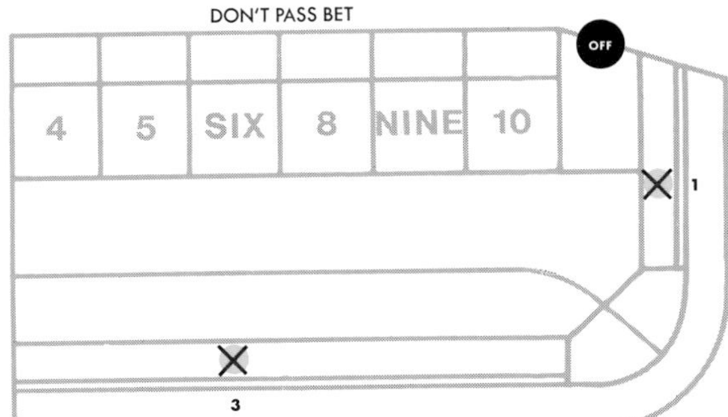

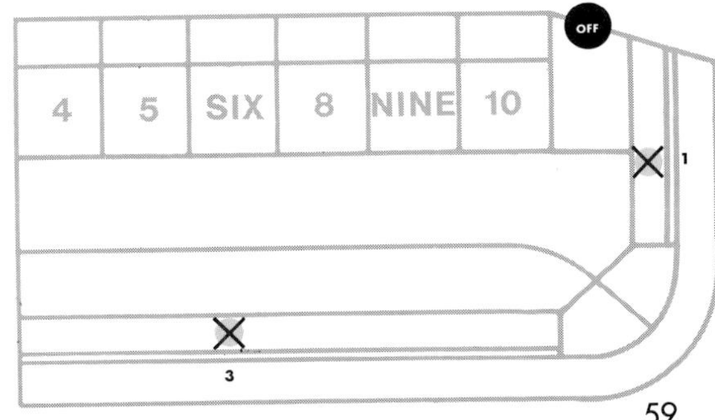

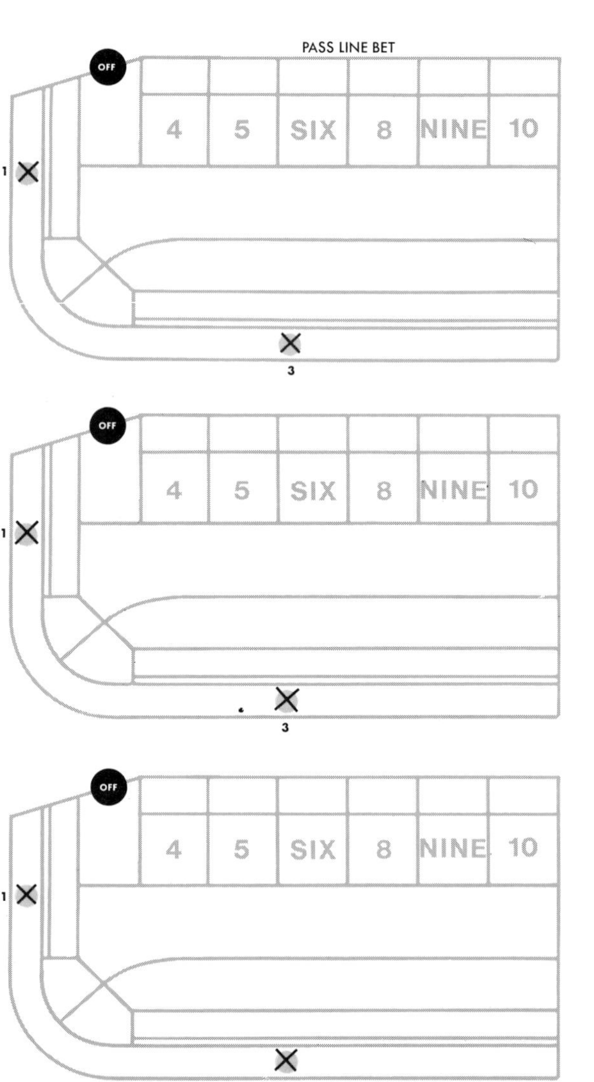
PASS LINE BET
OFF
4
5
SIX
8
NINE
10
1
3
PASS
OFF
4
5
SIX
8
NINE
10
1
3
PASS
OFF
4
5
SIX
8
NINE
10
1
3
PASS

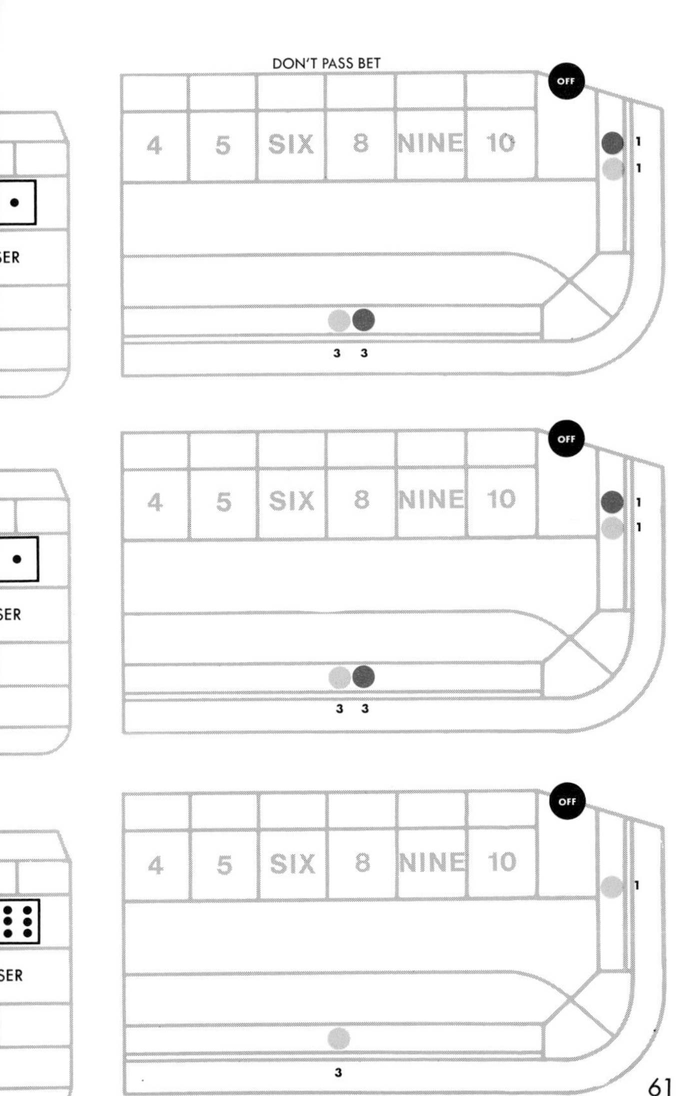
DON'T PASS BET
OFF
4
5
SIX
8
NINE
10
1
1
SER
3
3
OFF
4
5
SIX
8
NINE
10
1
1
SER
3
3
OFF
4
5
SIX
8
NINE
10
1
SER
3

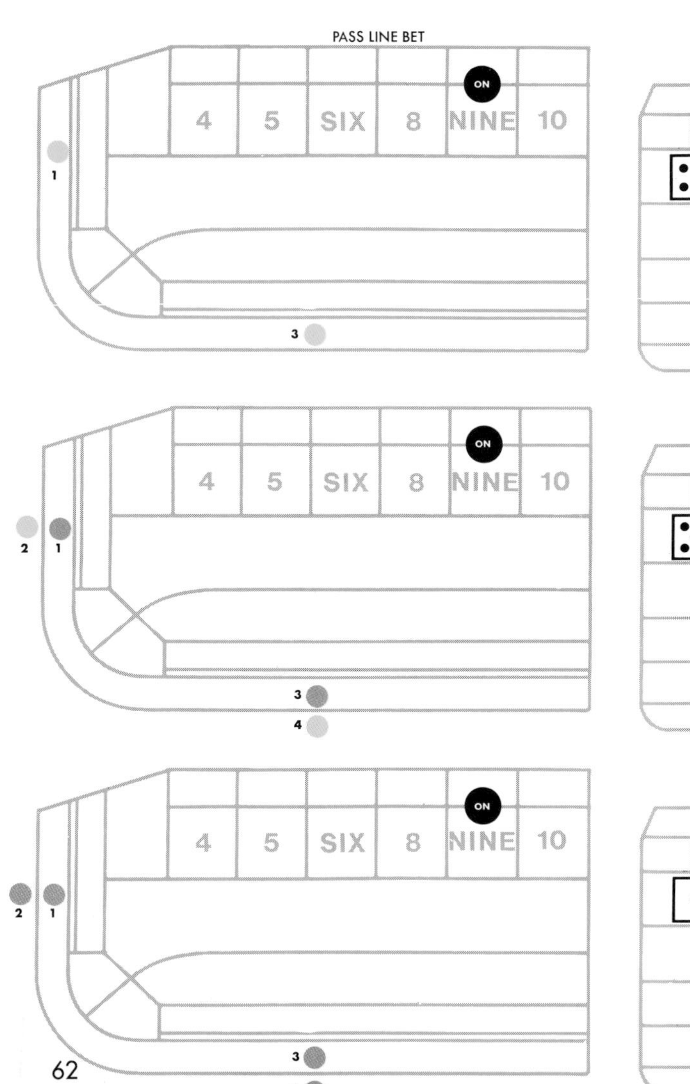
PASS LINE BET
ON
4
5
SIX
8
NINE
10
1
3
ON
4
5
SIX
8
NINE
10
2
1
3
4
ON
4
5
SIX
8
NINE
10
2
1
3
4

DON'T PASS BET

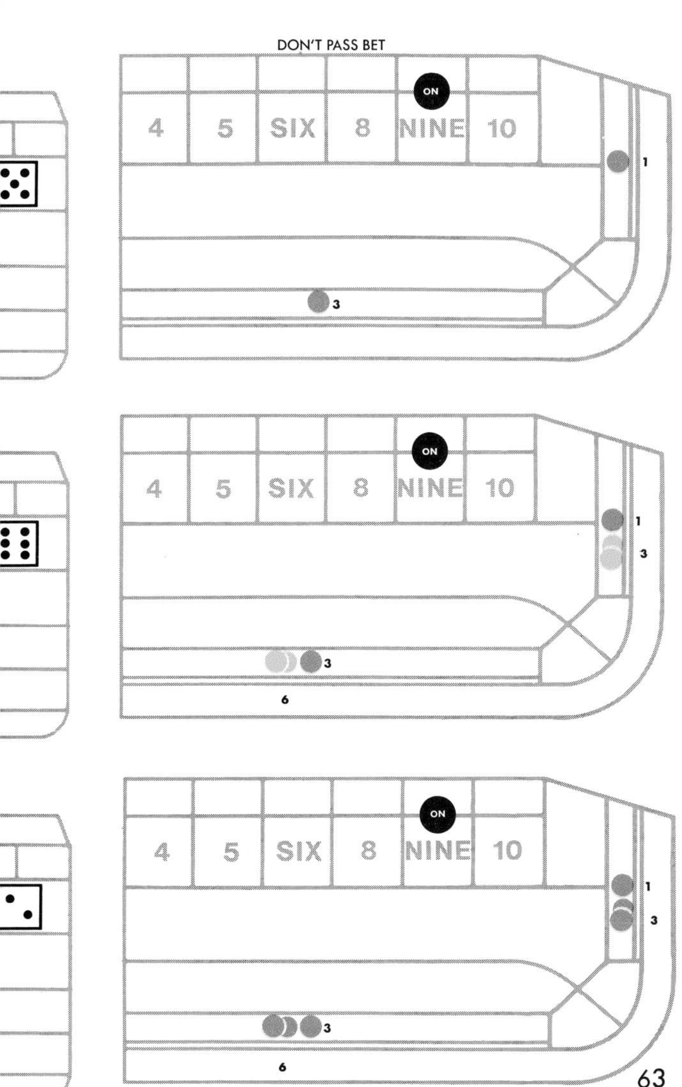

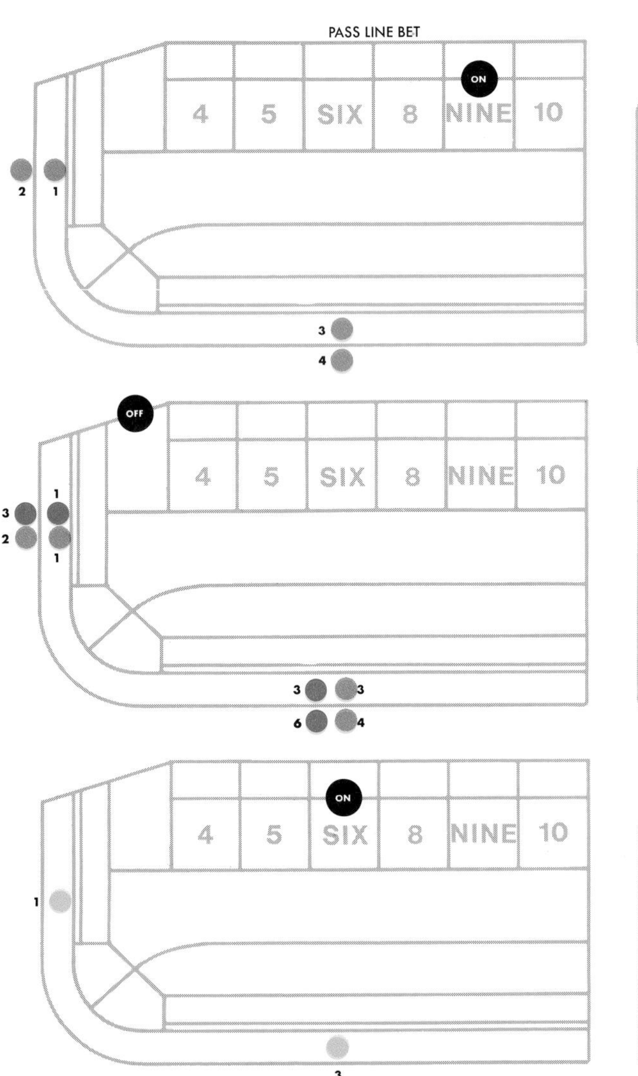

PASS LINE BET
ON
4
5
SIX
8
NINE
10
2
1
3
4
OFF
4
5
SIX
8
NINE
10
3
2
1
1
3
6
3
4
PASS L
ON
4
5
SIX
8
NINE
10
1
3

DON'T PASS BET
ON
4
5
SIX
8
NINE
10
1
3
3
6
OFF
4
5
SIX
8
NINE
10
1
3
WINNER
3
6
ON
4
5
SIX
8
NINE
10
1
3

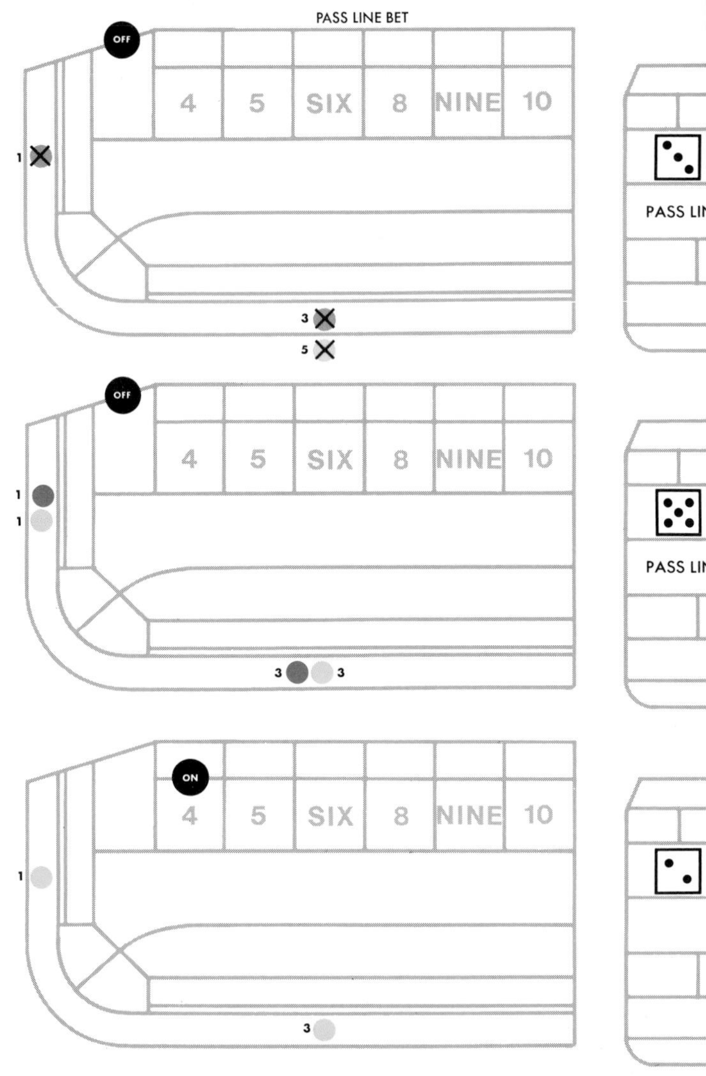
PASS LINE BET
OFF
4
5
SIX
8
NINE
10
1
3
5
PASS LIN
OFF
4
5
SIX
8
NINE
10
1
1
3
3
PASS LIN
ON
4
5
SIX
8
NINE
10
1
3

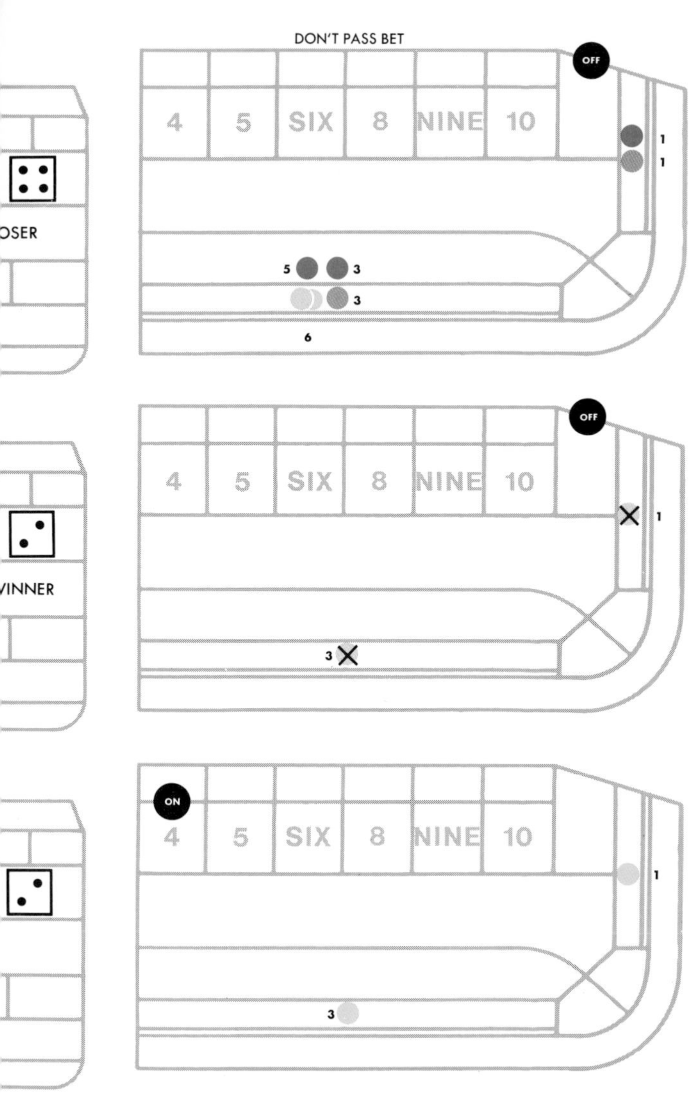
DON'T PASS BET
OFF
4
5
SIX
8
NINE
10
1
1
OSER
5
3
3
6
OFF
4
5
SIX
8
NINE
10
1
VINNER
3
ON
4
5
SIX
8
NINE
10
1
3

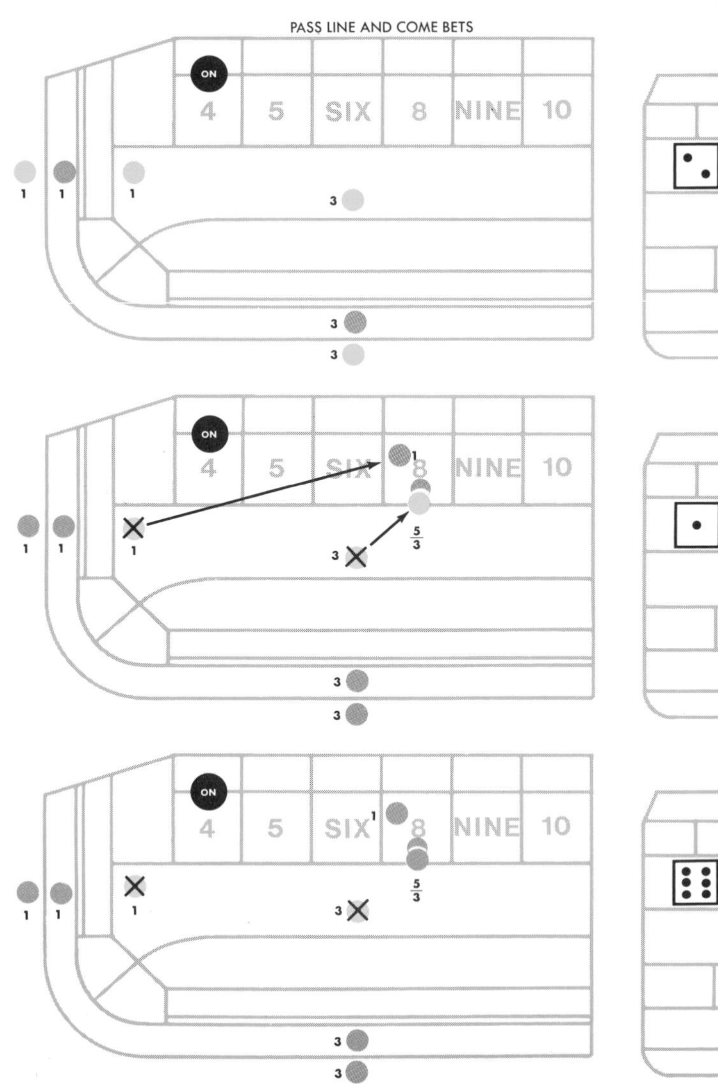
ON
4
5
SIX
8
NINE
10
1
1
1
3
3
3
ON
4
5
SIX
8
NINE
10
1
1
1
1
5
3
3
3
3
ON
4
5
SIX
8
NINE
10
1
1
1
1
5
3
3
3
3

DON'T PASS AND DON'T COME BETS

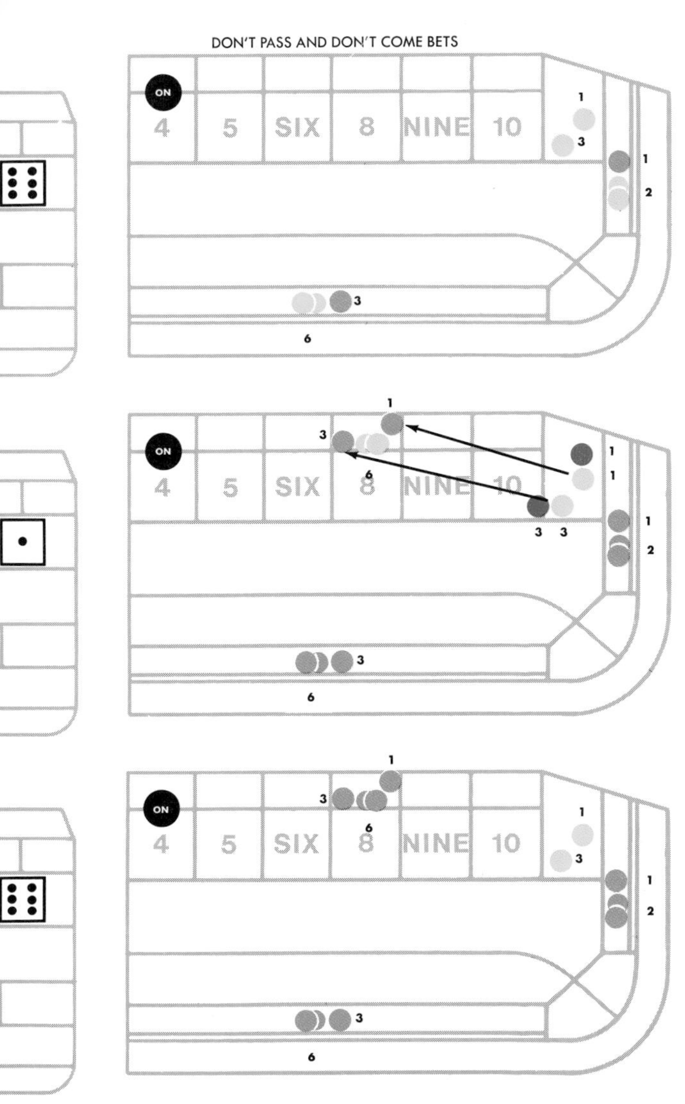

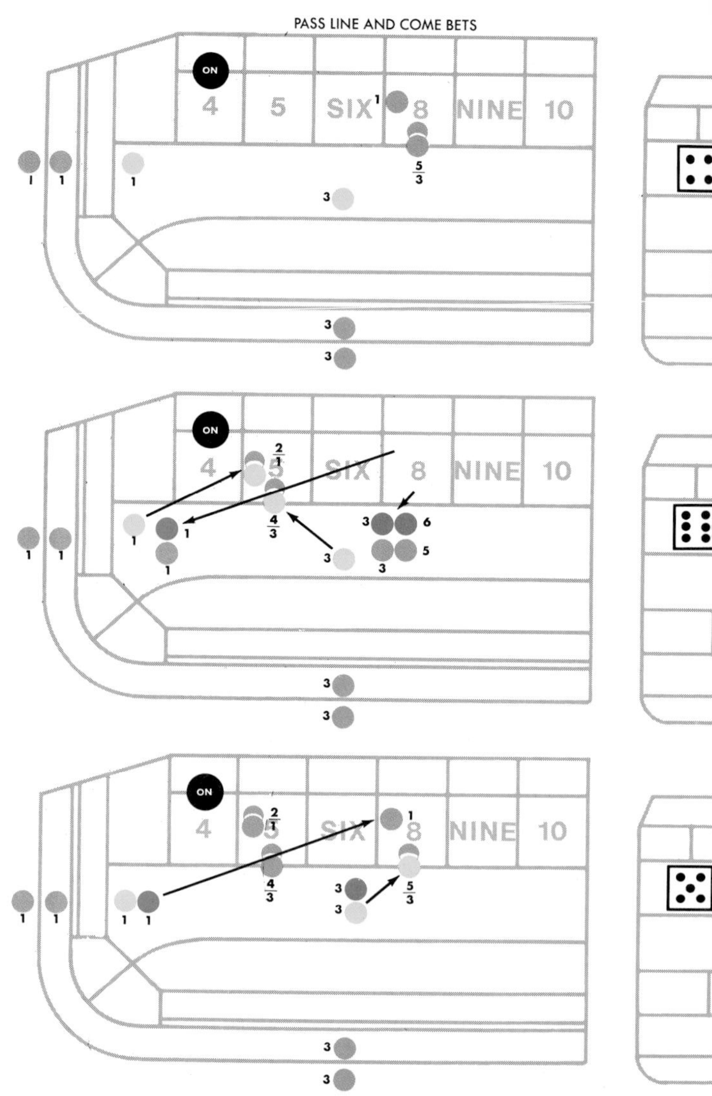
PASS LINE AND COME BETS
ON
4
5
SIX
8
NINE
10

DON'T PASS AND DON'T COME BETS

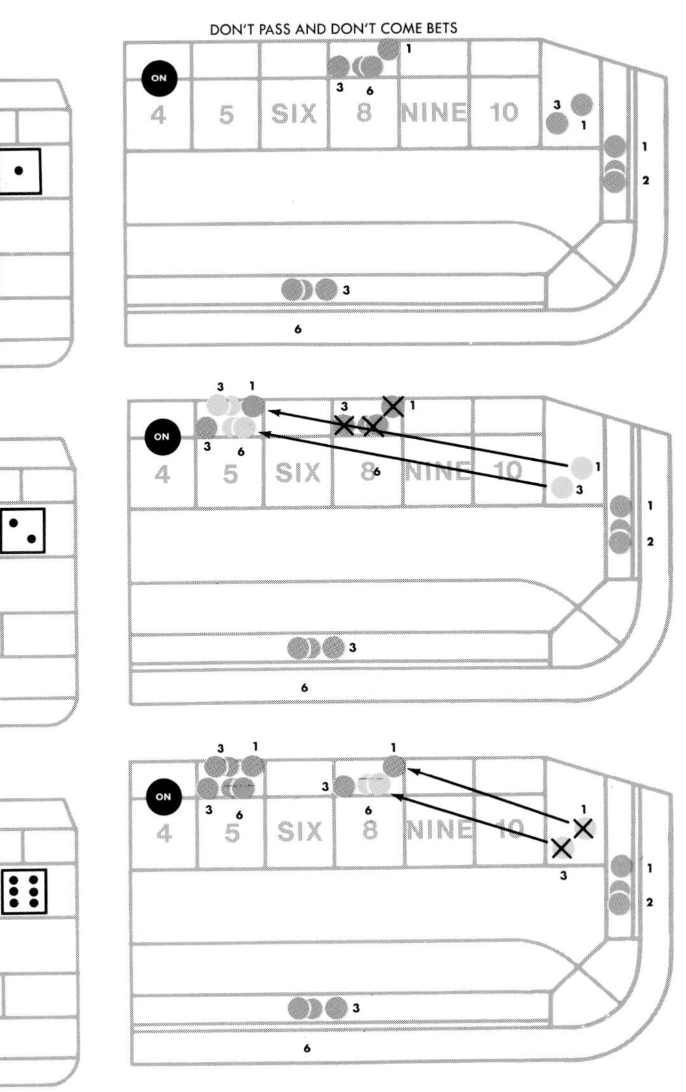

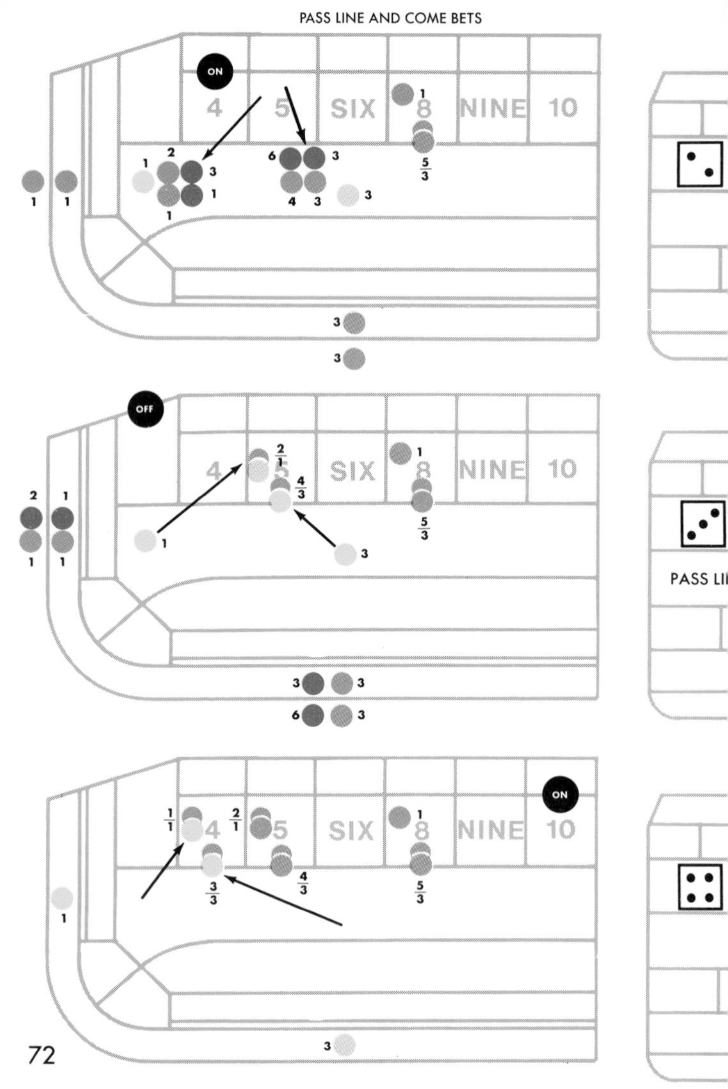
ON
4
5
SIX
8
NINE
10
OFF
PASS LI

DON'T PASS AND DON'T COME BETS

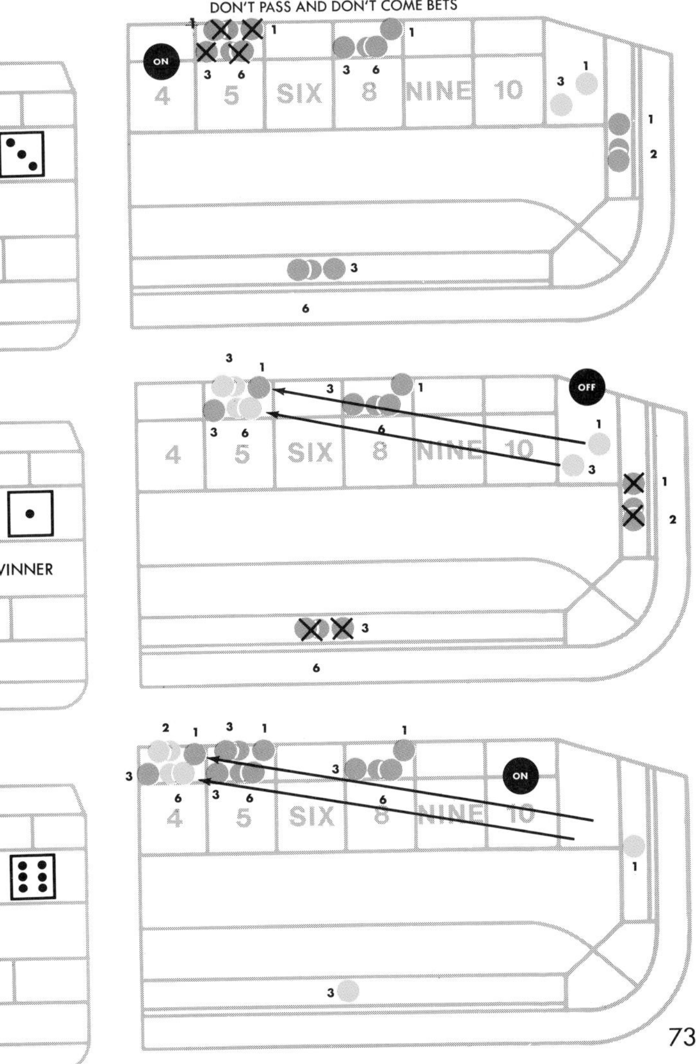

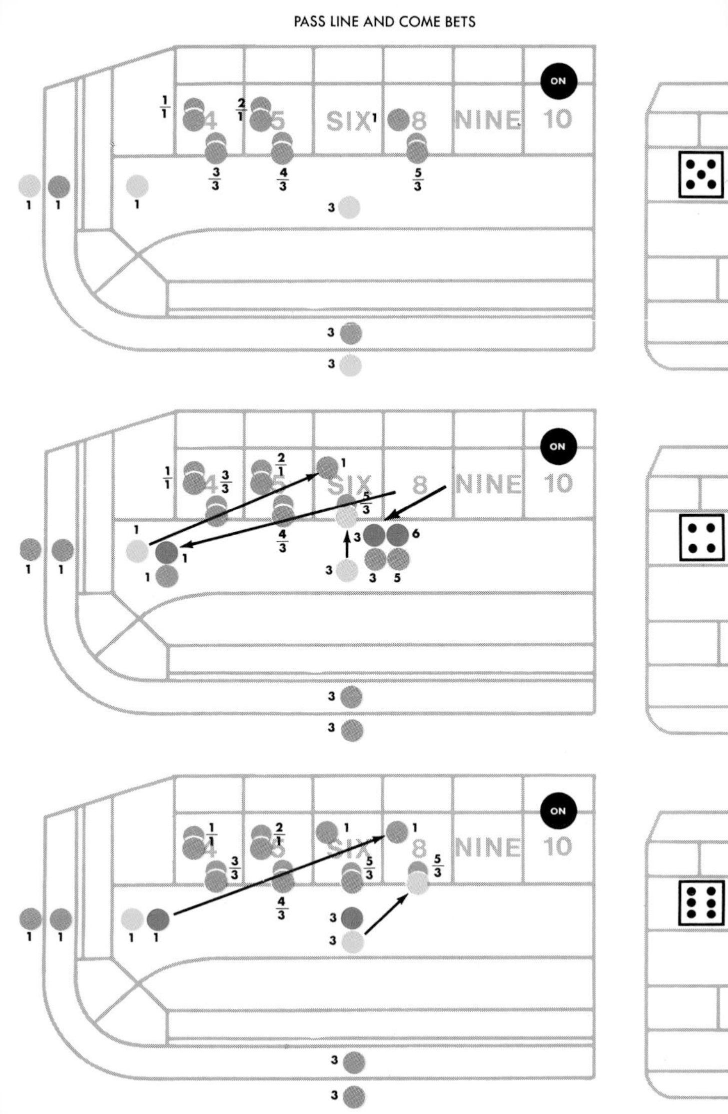
ON
4
5
SIX
8
NINE
10

DON'T PASS AND DON'T COME BETS

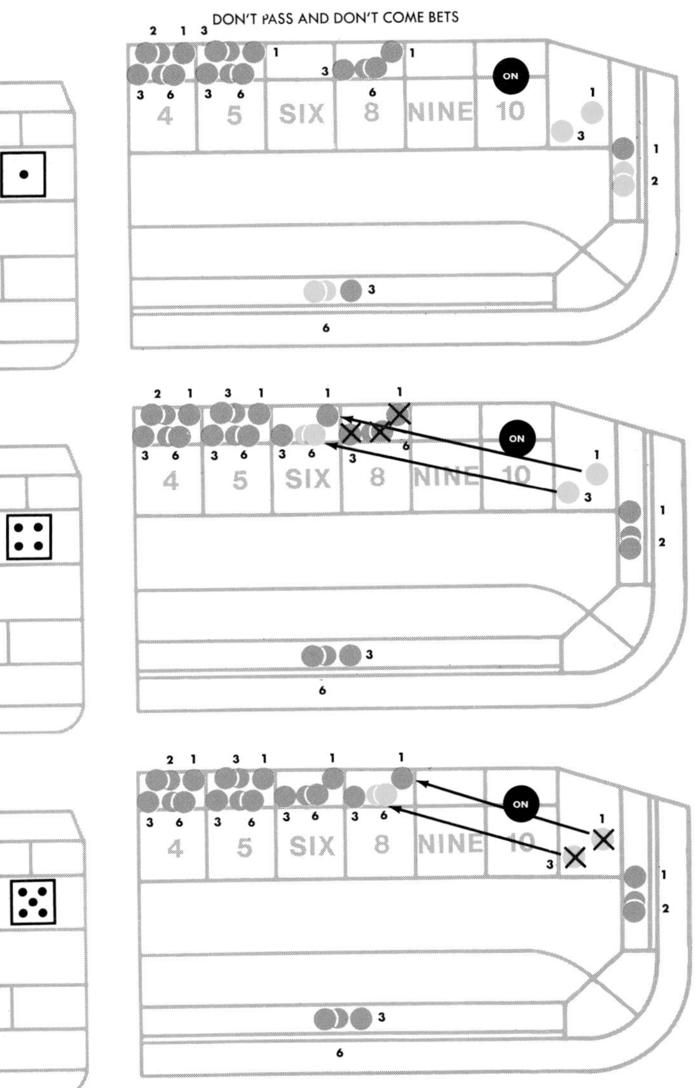

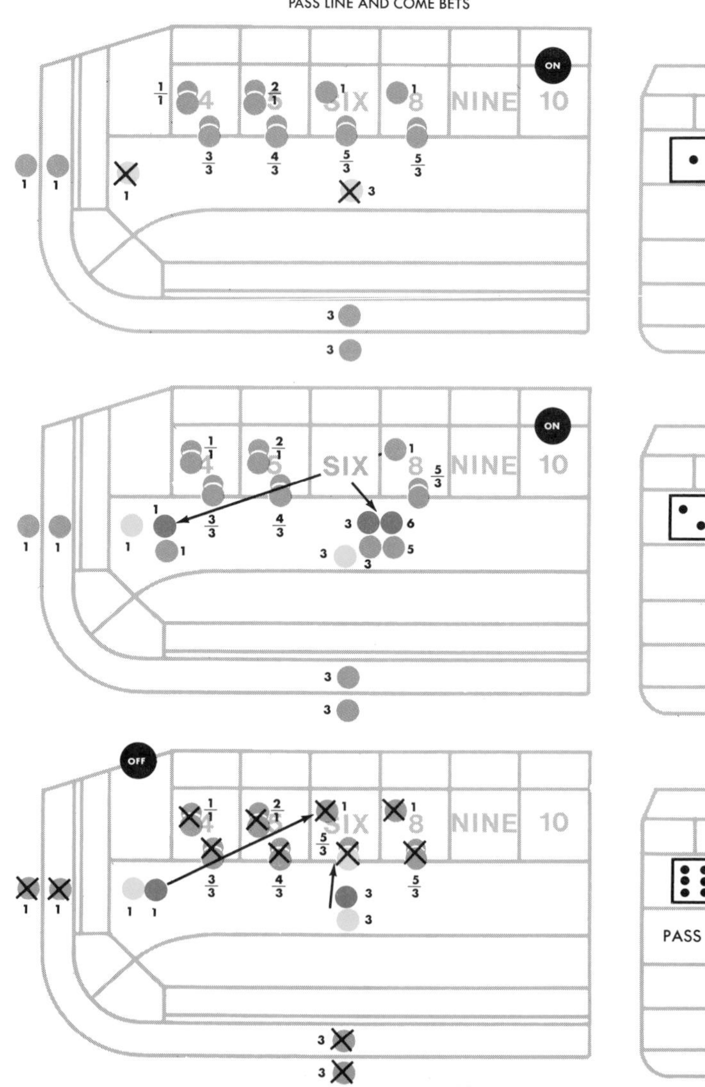
ON
SIX
NINE
10
ON
SIX
NINE
10
OFF
SIX
NINE
10
PASS L

4
5
SIX
8
NINE
10
ON
OFF
)SER

CASINO ADVANTAGE

DO's		DON'Ts	
Pass	1.414%	Don't Pass	1.402%
Come	1.414%	Don't Come	1.402%
Place 6 or 8	1.515%	Lay 4 or 10	2.439%
Place 5 or 9	4.000%	Lay 5 or 9	3.225%
Place 4 or 10	6.667%	Lay 6 or 8	4.000%

PROPOSITIONS			
Field (20 to 19)	2.778%	Any Craps	11.111%
Field (20 to 18)	5.556%	3 or 11 (15 to 1)	11.111%
Big 6 or Big 8	9.091%	3 or 11 (14 to 1)	16.667%
Hard 6 or Hard 8	9.091%	2 or 12 (30 to 1)	13.889%
Hard 4 or Hard 10	11.111%	2 or 12 (29 to 1)	16.667%
7	16.667%		

CRAPS BET PERCENTAGES—that is, the casino advantage for every Craps wager—are shown in the above chart. Because they have a higher casino advantage than the Pass, Come, Don't Pass, and Don't Come wagers, players are cautioned against taking any of the Craps wagers that are described in the rest of this chapter.

THE INDIVIDUAL POINT BETS Buy, Place, and Lay let players wager on the individual Point totals of their choice. The Buy and Place bets win when the Point appears and lose on 7. The Lay Bet, which is the exact opposite, wins on 7 and loses when the Point appears. A player who wants to make a Buy, Lay, or Place wager puts the chips on the layout, usually in the Come box, and announces the bet to the dealer, who then sets the wager in the correct box or boxes.

INDIVIDUAL POINT BETS

4	5	SIX	8	NINE	10

WHEN BUY, PLACE, OR LAY WAGERS WIN, the payoff chips are placed directly in front of the player. The player should immediately remove these chips from the Crap layout.

Wagers are made in specific multiples. When a wager wins and the player wants to double the amount of the wager, he or she says, "Press," which instructs the dealer to double the amount of a winning Buy or Place wager before giving the remainder of the payoff to the player. These bets may be wagered or removed on any roll. The phrase "Take down" instructs the dealer to remove these wagers, which the dealer will then set directly in front of the player.

The Buy and Place wagers, which are Do wagers because they win on the Point and lose on 7, are automatically "off" on Come-out rolls unless the dealer is informed that they are "working." When they work, the dealer sets either the Point marker or an "On" button on the player's wager.

The Lay wagers, which are Don't wagers, always work when they are on the layout. When a player calls a Lay wager "down," even for one roll, the wager must be removed from the table. Although a description of each of these three bets follows, it is advised that you not make them, because most have a relatively high casino advantage and require considerably more than $5—as much as $41—to wager them, as described in the next four pages.

THE BUY BETS have the same payoff ratio as the Odds Bets. The Odds Bets have no casino advantage, but a "Commission" charge of 5 percent of the player's total wager creates a casino advantage for the Buy Bets. The smallest Commission charge is $1, even at games that have a $5 minimum.

The casino Commission equals 5 percent because the wagers are made in multiples of $20. The $1 Commission is 5 percent of $20. Buy wagers are made in multiples of $21—$20 for the wager and $1 for the Commission. Therefore, the casino advantage is 4.762 percent and not 5 percent because the player loses an average of $1 for every $21 wagered.

Casinos will permit wagers of less than $20, but this increases the casino advantage because the full Commission must be paid for each multiple or partial multiple of $20 or less. For example, a $1 Commission on a $10 Buy wager increases the casino advantage from 4.762 percent to 9.09 percent. However, some casinos will allow players to make Buy wagers of $25 for a Commission of only $1, thus reducing the casino advantage to 3.85 percent.

BUY

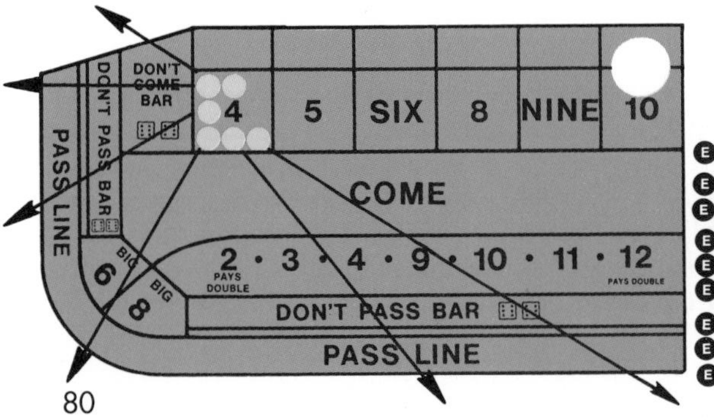

A SMALL "BUY" BUTTON is put on the wager to show it is to be paid according to the Odds ratio and not 1 to 1, as a Come wager would be. If the Point appears, the player wins, and he or she either takes the original wager down with the winnings or pays the 5 percent Commission again for the next roll. If the player removes the Buy wager before it wins or loses, the dealer returns the Commission. On Come-out rolls, Buy wagers are automatically off.

BUY BET PAYOFFS

Point	Payoff	Odds Ratio
4 or 10	40 to 20	2 to 1
5 or 9	30 to 20	3 to 2
6 or 8	24 to 20	6 to 5

A player may "buy" any single Point or any combination of Points on any roll. The player makes a Buy wager by setting the wager on the layout and calling out the Point that is wanted. The dealer removes the Commission for the casino while putting the wager in the correct Point box. The wager is set in the Point box in the same way as a Come wager.

BET

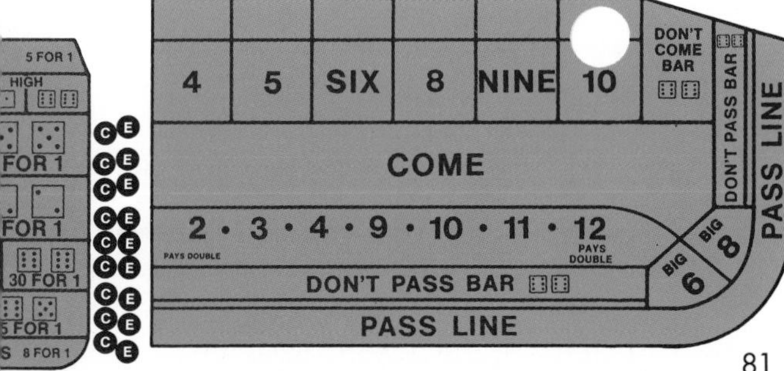

LAY BETS are the opposite of Buy Bets because they win on 7 and lose when the Point appears. Lay wagers are made in multiples of the payoffs for the Buy wager—$24, $30, and $40.

Lay wagers win in multiples of $20. The 5 percent Commission for Lay wagers is paid on the amount of the payoff, whereas the 5 percent Commission for Buy wagers is paid on the amount of the wager. Thus the Commission for both of these wagers is always paid on multiples of $20.

THE COMMISSION ON LAY WAGERS is based on the payoff. For example, if the player lays the Point 4 for $40 to win $20, he or she pays only a $1, not a $2, Commission. This is only 2.44 percent of the $41 wager and Commission. The casino advantage for Lay wagers is less than the 4.762 percent for Buy wagers. The casino advantage for 4 and 10 is 2.44 percent, 5 and 9 is 3.23 percent, and 6 and 8 is 4.00 percent.

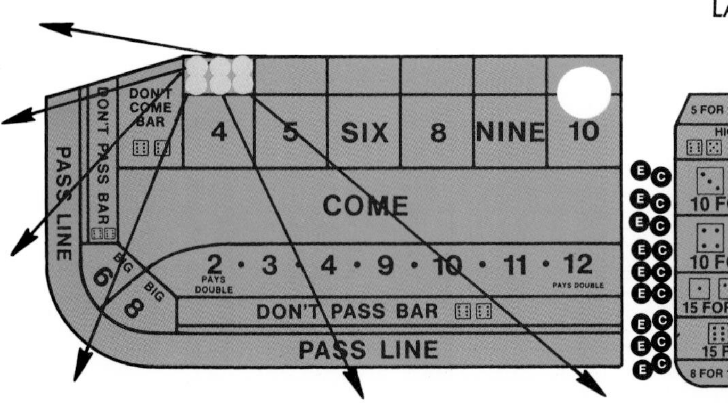

The player makes a Lay wager by setting the bet on the layout and calling out the Point or Points he or she desires. The dealer removes the Commission for the casino as the wager is put into the correct Don't Point box. The dealer then puts a small "Lay" button on top of the wager to indicate it is to be paid according to the Odds ratio and not 1 to 1, as a Don't Come wager would be.

LAY BET PAYOFFS

Point	Payoff	Odds Ratio
4 or 10	20 to 40	1 to 2
5 or 9	20 to 30	2 to 3
6 or 8	20 to 24	5 to 6

If a 7 appears, the player wins. The original wager must be taken down with the winnings or the 5 percent Commission paid again for the next roll.

If the player decides to remove the Lay wager before it wins or loses, the dealer also returns the Commission. Lay wagers work on every roll.

BET

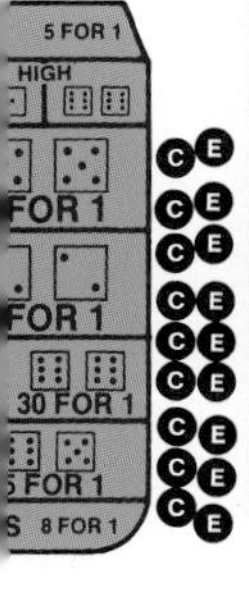

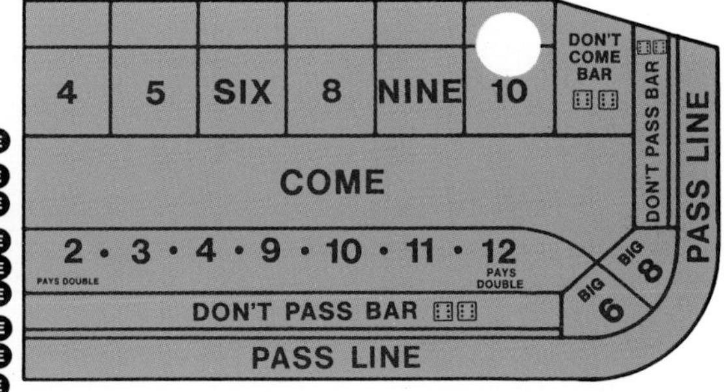

PLACE WAGERS can be made on any Point or on any combination of Points on any roll. A player makes a Place wager by putting the bet down on the layout and calling out the Points wanted. The dealer then puts the wager on the line above or below the Come Point box in Las Vegas and most other jurisdictions and in the Place Point box in Reno-Tahoe. In both cases the wager is placed according to the player's table location. Place wagers can be removed on any roll; they are automatically off on Come-out rolls.

Place Bets, depending on the Point, require wagers in multiples of \$5 or \$6. Like Buy Bets, they can be wagered for less, but this increases the casino advantage.

PLACE POINTS 6 and 8 have the least casino advantage of all the Place Bets and are the best wagers to make next to the Do and Don't wagers, Pass and Come. Points 4 and 10 have the highest casino advantage of the Place Bets, and the 6.67 percent casino advantage is greater than the 4.76 percent for Buy Bets of the same Points. In terms of casino advantage, the Points 5,

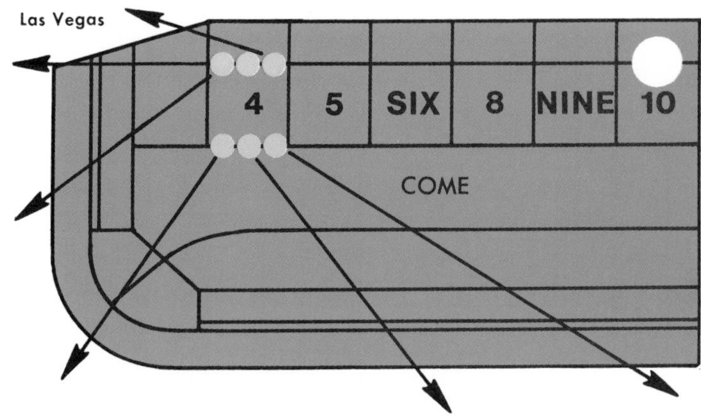

PAYOFFS are based on the Odds ratios plus a 1 to 1 wager. The 1 to 1 wager of 1 unit creates the casino advantage because Place Bets do not win as often as they lose. For example, with Point 6 the Odds ratio is 6 to 5, so 1 unit is added to each side of the ratio to create a payoff of 7 to 6 units.

PLACE BET PAYOFFS

Point	Payoff	Odds Ratio
4 or 10	9 to 5	8 to 4
5 or 9	7 to 5	6 to 4
6 or 8	7 to 6	6 to 5

6, 8, and 9 should be placed rather than bought, but 4 and 10 should be bought if the player can afford the $21 minimum instead of the $5 minimum required to place them. There are several popular ways of choosing the Points to be placed, but none alters the casino advantage. The two "inside" Points of 6 and 8 are the best Place Bets. The four inside Points of 5, 6, 8, and 9 are also wagered together. A "5 across" means that all the Points except the one with the Point marker are wagered in multiples of $26 or $27, depending on the Pass Line Point. A "6 across" means all six Points are placed and wagered in multiples of $32.

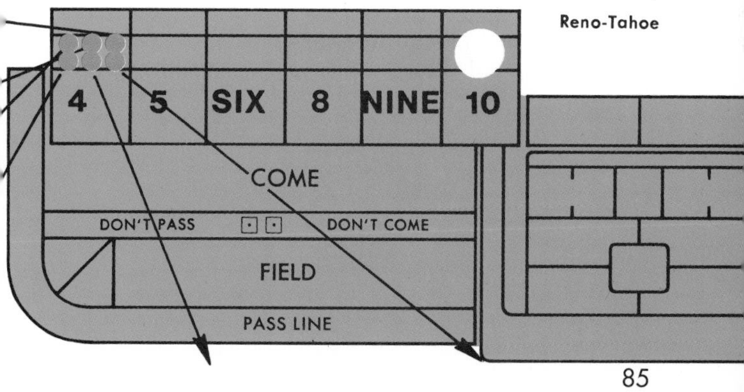

Sometimes only the single Point opposite the Pass Line Point is bet. The opposite Points are 4 and 10 = 14, 5 and 9 = 14, and 6 and 8 = 14 because these are the combinations on the opposite sides of the dice. The total on the top of the dice and the total on the bottom of the dice always add up to 14.

PLACE vs. BUY BETS

	4	5	6	8	9	10
Place	6.67%	4.00%	1.52%	1.52%	4.00%	6.67%
Buy	4.76%	4.76%	4.76%	4.76%	4.76%	4.76%

BIG 6 AND BIG 8 wagers are set in position by the player. Each wins if the Point appears (in this example, a 6) and loses on 7. The dealer pays 1 to 1 and puts the winnings next to the player's wager. Both the wager and the payoff remain for the next roll unless the player changes the amount or removes them. Big 6 and Big 8 have the highest casino advantage, 9.091 percent, of all wagers on the outside sections of the layout. On the average, Big 6 and Big 8 lose six times faster than placing 6 and 8, with 1.52 percent, and twice as fast

BIG AND BIG BETS

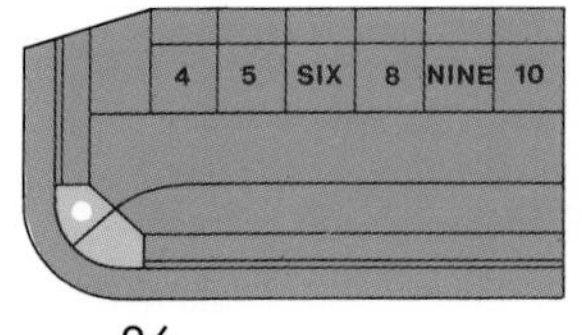

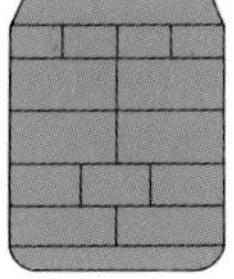

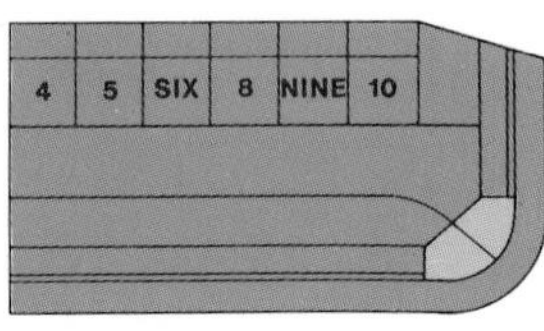

as buying 6 and 8, with 4.76 percent. For example, the player wins only 1 to 1, which is also 6 to 6, on the Big 6, but wins 7 to 6 by placing 6.

THE FIELD BET is also set in position by the player. The bet wins or loses on every roll. The player wins if any of the seven totals printed in the Field appears and loses if any of the other four totals, 5, 6, 7, or 8, appears.

In the Field Bet, the casino's four totals appear more often than the player's seven totals, so all jurisdictions pay 1 to 1 if 3, 4, 9, 10, or 11 is rolled and 2 to 1 if 2 or 12 is rolled. The numbers that pay more than even money are circled.

The Reno-Tahoe and downtown Las Vegas casinos increase the payoff on either 2 or 12 to 3 to 1 to reduce the Strip's advantage from 5.56 percent to 2.78 percent. Though this is still a relatively high percentage, it makes this bet more desirable than the rest of the bets on the layout with the exception of the Pass Line, Come, Don't Pass, Don't Come, Place 6 and Place 8, and Lay 4 and Lay 10.

Casinos in other areas of the world often have other payoff combinations, and sometimes the casino advantage is increased. The dealer puts the payoff next to the player's wager, and both stacks of chips remain for the next roll unless the player removes them or makes another change.

FIELD BET

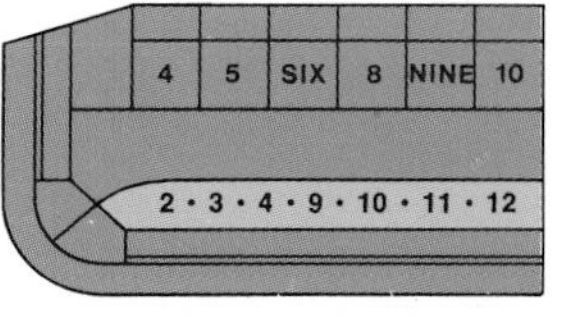

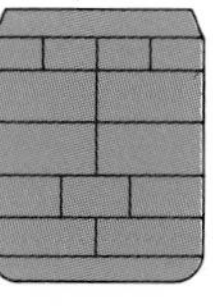
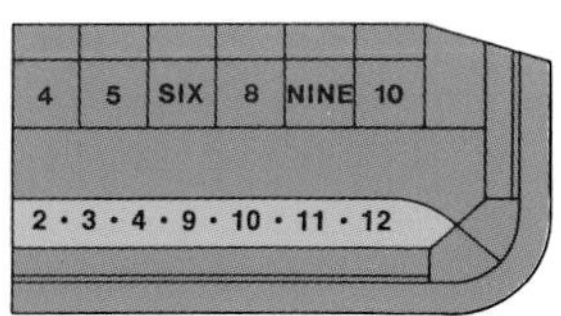

PROPOSITION BETS are handled by the Stickman, who also controls the dice. A player makes a wager on a Proposition Bet by tossing chips into the center of the layout while announcing the wager and the amount—for example, "Two dollar eleven." The Stickman places the wager in the stated box unless busy with the dice or other Proposition Bets. Then the Stickman, Boxman, or dealer calls out the player's wager, which wins or loses on the next roll no matter where the chips lie.

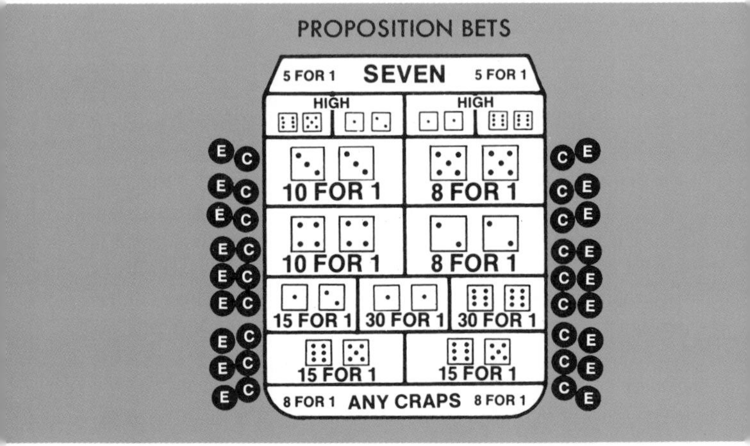

PROPOSITION BETS

THE STICKMAN places the wager in the Proposition betting box according to the player's table location. If the wager wins, the Stickman points out the winning player and announces the payoff to the dealer, who sets it in front of the player.

Proposition Bet payoffs do not include the amount of the player's wager; this is left in the Proposition betting box for the next roll. At any time players may direct the Stickman to "take down" the wager and return it to them.

Proposition Bets have a picture of the only winning dice combination and the amount of the payoff listed in each box.

CUSTOMER-PROPOSITION BET LOCATION

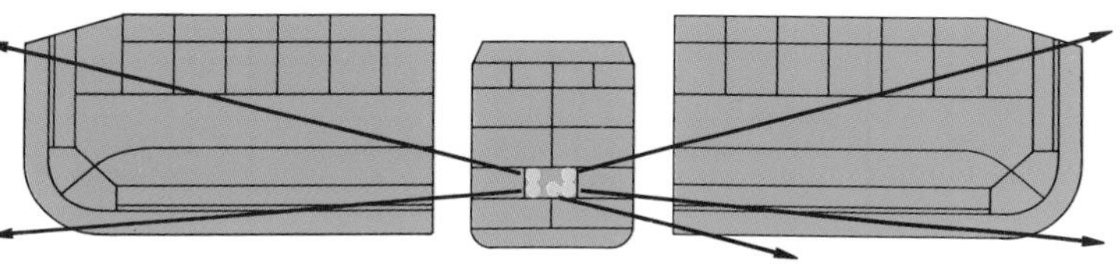

One-roll Proposition Bets are wagered only for the next roll of the dice. They win if the dice combination pictured in the box appears but lose if any other combination appears.

Players generally make One-roll wagers only on Come-out rolls because they contain the five totals that win (Natural 7 and 11) and lose (Craps 2, 3, and 12), but any one of these totals or any combination of them can be wagered at any time. Note that when a 7 appears, every wager on the layout either wins or loses; this clears the table of wagers.

ONE ROLL BETS

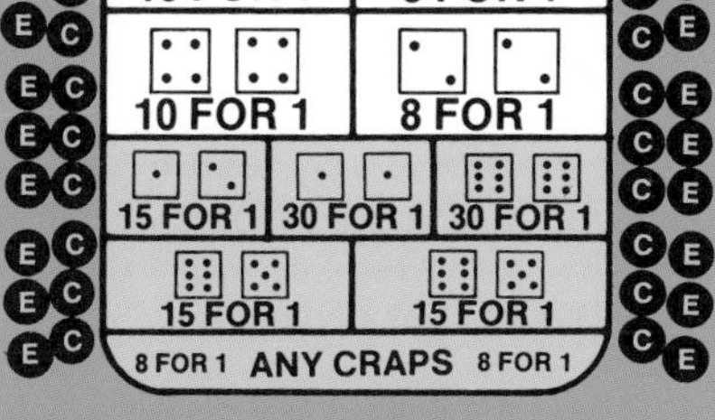

5 FOR 1 SEVEN 5 FOR 1

HIGH HIGH

10 FOR 1 8 FOR 1

10 FOR 1 8 FOR 1

15 FOR 1 30 FOR 1 30 FOR 1

15 FOR 1 15 FOR 1

8 FOR 1 ANY CRAPS 8 FOR 1

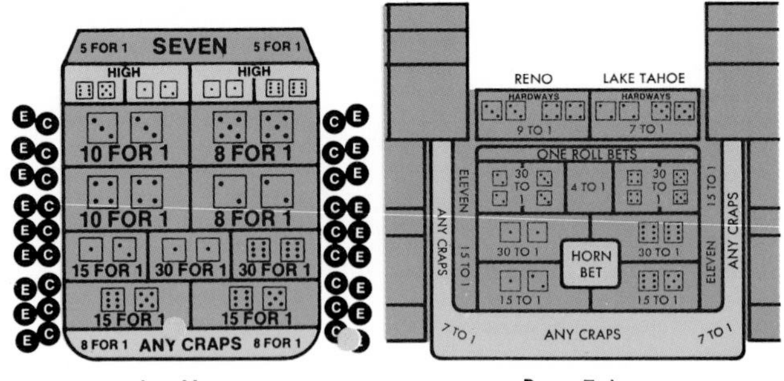

Las Vegas

Reno-Tahoe

"ANY CRAPS" involves the three Craps numbers 2, 3, and 12. Any Craps wins if any of these totals appears. Eleven, Craps, and the combination of Craps-Eleven are the most popular Proposition Bets. The Stickman sets Craps-Eleven wagers either on the line separating the two bets or between the Craps and Eleven circles at the edge of the Proposition Bets pointing to the player locations.

THE HORN BET is a combination of the Any Craps (2, 3, and 12) and 11. It must be wagered in multiples of $4 and pays off according to each individual total minus the three chips wagered on the other three totals, which lost.

Horn High wagers are five-unit wagers with one unit on each of three numbers and two units on the fourth. They pay off according to the individual totals. For three of the totals this would be the individual payoff minus the four losing chips, but for the fourth total this would be twice the individual payoff minus the three losing chips.

The Whirl wager of all five Come-out totals (2, 3, 7, 11, and 12) is rarely made.

"TO" AND "FOR" are important words in gambling payoff ratios; it is important to distinguish between them. The word "to" indicates the player wins the payoff and also receives the amount of the original wager. The word "for" indicates that the player wins only the payoff total. The player wins one unit less when "for" is used instead of "to." "For" is found primarily on the Las Vegas Strip.

PAYOFFS

TO	vs	FOR
Stated Payoff		Actual Amount
8 to 1		8 + 1 = 9
8 for 1		8 + 0 = 8

The payoffs for One-roll wagers vary from casino to casino. Most Reno-Tahoe and downtown Las Vegas casinos pay one chip more than do the Strip casinos for the totals 2, 3, 11, and 12. Because they are based on these four individual payoffs, this difference also affects Horn wagers.

HOP BETS are One-roll wagers that a single dice combination will appear on the next roll, or "Hop," of the dice. The Reno-Tahoe layout, which is shown below, has a One-roll wager for each of the four even-numbered Points. Some casinos will let customers make Hop wagers for any dice combination of their choosing.

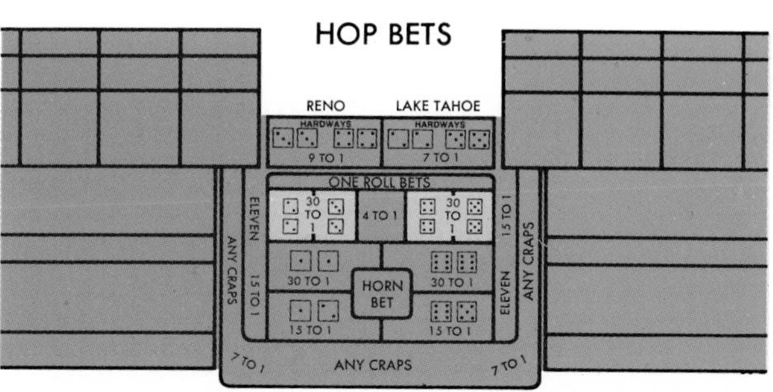

HOP BET POSSIBILITIES

2	3	4	5	6	7	8	9	10	11	12
1 + 1	1 + 2	1 + 3	1 + 4	1 + 5	1 + 6					
		2 + 2	2 + 3	2 + 4	2 + 5	2 + 6				
				3 + 3	3 + 4	3 + 5	3 + 6			
						4 + 4	4 + 5	4 + 6		
								5 + 5	5 + 6	
										6 + 6

The player may wager that any of the possible dice combinations (shown above) will appear on the next roll, or Hop, of the dice. A Hop wager loses unless the designated combination appears.

To make a Hop wager, the player tosses the chips to the Boxman and calls out the dice combination. The Boxman repeats the call while putting the wager in the blank area of the layout directly in front of him or her. Hop wagers are paid off according to the ratios for the printed One-roll Bets, which have the same probability of occurrence (these ratios vary from casino to casino). The six possible pairs are each paid off the same as a pair of 1's or 6's, and the fifteen possible dice combinations made up of different numbers—for example, a 9 (4 and 5)—are each paid off the same as would be a 3 (1 and 2) or 11 (5 and 6). The four totals of 5 and 9, no matter what combination creates them, and Easy 6 and 8 are paid off the same as with Any Craps.

HARD vs. EASY COMBINATIONS

Total	Hard Way	Easy Way
4	2 2	1 3
6	3 3	1 5 and 2 4
8	4 4	3 5 and 2 6
10	5 5	4 6

HARDWAY BETS

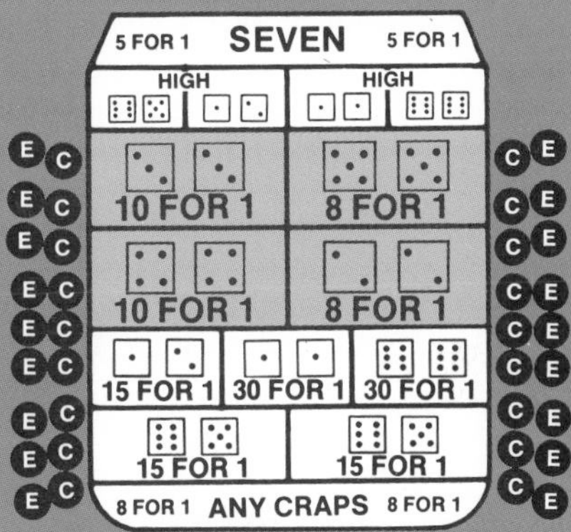

The Hard 6 and Hard 8 bets pay 10 for 1 while the Hard 4 and Hard 10 bets pay only 8 for 1, because there are more easy combinations that make the Hard 6 and Hard 8 lose.

HARDWAY PROPOSITIONS, involving the Point totals 4, 6, 8, and 10, are usually made after a Point has been established, to increase the amount bet on it. "Hardway" means a pair of the same number. The player wins if a "Hard" combination appears, such as 2 and 2 for Hard 4, and loses when either a 7 or an "Easy" combination of the total appears, such as 1 and 3 for Easy 4. The wager is affected only when a 7 or the Hard or Easy combinations for the total appear on a roll. Hardways have a lower casino advantage than do other Proposition Bets, but they still have a casino advantage several times greater than the recommended wagers. In Las Vegas and most other areas, Hardways work on the Come-out roll, but not in New Jersey.

KENO

The game of Keno uses the numbers 1 through 80, which are printed on tickets that are placed throughout the Keno lounge or any other area that has been made available to players, such as dining rooms, bars, and casino. The players may select from one to fifteen of

A typical Keno counter is shown below.

these numbers on which to wager. Then the casino selects at random twenty of the eighty available numbers. The amount won depends on the ratio of the player's matching choices to those selected at random by the casino. As an example, payoffs in Nevada can exceed $100,000 and be won with a wager of only a few dollars.

A standard unmarked Keno ticket is shown below.

FIRST GAME	NO. OF GAMES	TOTAL PRICE
LAST GAME		

1	2	3	4	5	6	7	8	9	10	PRICE PER GAME
11	12	13	14	15	16	17	18	19	20	
21	22	23	24	25	26	27	28	29	30	
31	32	33	34	35	36	37	38	39	40	

MULTI GAME KENO FROM 2 TO 1000 GAMES IN ADVANCE

41	42	43	44	45	46	47	48	49	50
51	52	53	54	55	56	57	58	59	60
61	62	63	64	65	66	67	68	69	70
71	72	73	74	75	76	77	78	79	80

WIN UP TO $200,000 OR MORE

PRICE AND PAYOFF SCHEDULE

MARK ANY 4 NUMBERS			
Catch	**Bet 1.00**	**Bet 2.00**	**Bet 5.00**
2 Wins	1.00	2.00	5.00
3 Wins	3.00	6.00	15.00
4 Wins	125.00	250.00	625.00

MARK ANY 8 NUMBERS			
Catch	**Bet 1.00**	**Bet 2.00**	**Bet 5.00**
5 Wins	9.00	18.00	45.00
6 Wins	90.00	180.00	450.00
7 Wins	1,495.00	2,990.00	7,475.00
8 Wins	25,000.00	50,000.00	50,000.00

TICKET PRICES are contained in brochures that are usually found with the blank Keno tickets. These brochures list both the prices and the payoff schedules for the different types of tickets that can be purchased. The illustration above shows the prices and payoffs for a 4-spot and an 8-spot ticket.

Most tickets have a minimum wager of $1 or $2, although some casinos offer special rates. Tickets may be purchased in multiples of the minimum price; the payoffs are increased by similar multiples. For example, if the minimum price of a ticket is $1 and the player wagers $2 or $5, the respective payoffs are increased two or five times the basic payoff schedule.

FIRST GAME	NO. OF GAMES	TOTAL PRICE
LAST GAME		$1^{\underline{00}}$
		PRICE PER GAME

1	2	3	4	5	6	7	8	9	X
11	12	13	14	15	16	17	18	X	20
21	22	23	24	25	26	27	28	29	30
31	32	33	X	35	36	37	38	39	40

8

MULTI GAME KENO FROM 2 TO 1000 GAMES IN ADVANCE

X	42	43	X	45	46	47	48	X	50
51	X	53	54	55	56	57	58	59	60
61	62	63	64	65	66	67	68	69	70
X	72	73	74	75	76	77	78	79	80

WIN UP TO $200,000 OR MORE

A COMPLETED KENO TICKET shows the player's choices and the price of the ticket. The player indicates those choices by placing an X over the desired numbers using a black crayon provided with the ticket. Players may select from one to fifteen and sometimes more of the eighty numbers. They then write down the number of choices made (in this example, eight) on the right side of the ticket. They also write the price of the ticket (the amount being wagered) in the space designated for that purpose. Dollar signs and decimal points are never used. In the sample shown, the price is $1 for the ticket. If the price is $1 or more, the cents are underlined ($1^{\underline{00}}$, $1^{\underline{40}}$, $5^{\underline{00}}$, etc.).

BUYING KENO TICKETS is simply a matter of going to the windows located at the Keno counter (see photograph on page 94) and giving the marked ticket or tickets to a Keno "writer" along with the total purchase price. The Keno writer keeps the customer's original ticket and the money for the purchase price. The writer makes a copy of the customer's ticket and gives the customer the duplicate. This must be retained for the player to be paid if the ticket wins. The writer also gives the customer any change that is owed.

DATE	TIME	RATE	MULTI	TOTAL PRICE
Dec 23, 1995	8:39 PM	1.00		$1.00

REPLAY #	ACCOUNT #	1st GAME	LAST	WRITER	SERIAL #
		742		50	2-12811

1	2	3	4	5	6	7	8	9	10 X
11	12	13	14	15	16	17	18	19 X	20
21	22	23	24	25	26	27	28	29	30
31	32	33	34 X	35	36	37	38	39	40

1/8 1.00

MULTI GAME KENO FROM 2 TO 1000 GAMES IN ADVANCE

41 X	42	43	44 X	45	46	47	48	49 X	50
51	52 X	53	54	55	56	57	58	59	60
61	62	63	64	65	66	67	68	69	70
71 X	72	73	74	75	76	77	78	79	80

WEST GAME

The duplicate is identical to the original marked ticket except that it has the game number printed on it. The customer can win only on the game with the number that appears on the copy, which is the next game to be called.

Players should always check to be absolutely sure that the duplicate copy they receive is correct. This is because casinos will pay off only according to the numbers which are stored in the computer for later verification.

TWENTY WINNING NUMBERS are selected at random from a clear plastic bowl or metal cage called a "goose" or—far more common nowadays—by a computer. The goose contains eighty balls that are numbered from 1 through 80. All of the balls are mixed by an air current, and twenty balls are blown, one at a time, into the two "rabbit ears" at the top of the goose. In some casinos the goose rotates, and a random ball is forced into the rabbit ears on each rotation. The caller announces the number of each ball over the Keno lounge address system as the ball enters the rabbit ears.

The picture to the right shows Keno balls in the goose as they are blown up into the rabbit ears. The numbers on these balls are lit up on the Keno board in the background.

KENO BOARDS are located in the Keno lounge and are often also located in other parts of the casino, such as in certain restaurant and bar areas. This arrangement allows the Keno player to leave or to not be in the Keno lounge at all and still have a chance to play the game.

The big board prominently displays the game number that is currently being played, as well as the full eighty numbers. As each number is called it is lit up on the Keno board. These numbers once corresponded to Ping-Pong-like Keno balls sitting in a plastic goose or birdcage. Twenty balls would pop up at random, and as each was drawn out of the hopper, its number would be displayed on the Keno board. Today, computers are used in the majority of the games across the country.

These same twenty numbers are also punched into blank tickets that have the game number printed on them. Such draw tickets are used by both the employees and the players to quickly determine and verify winning tickets.

Because the draw ticket and the player's ticket are identical in size and overall form, when the draw ticket is placed over the player's original ticket or a duplicate copy of that ticket, the marks on the winning numbers that were selected by the player will show through the punched holes. If a player is in doubt about which numbers have been drawn, he or she can request that a draw ticket be placed over the ticket that is in question for quick verification.

Keno is derived from a 2,000-year-old game played in China based on a 1,000-word-long poem. When the game was introduced in Nevada with the present 80 numbers, it was associated with horse racing. Jockey numbers and horse names were called out. Until the early 1950s, the game was often called "Race Horse Keno." Later, the horse-racing aspect was eliminated.

PAYOFF SCHEDULES for winning tickets are listed in the Keno brochures along with prices for the standard 1- to 15-spot tickets. Although there are variations in payoffs between states, in each locale there is general conformity among casinos.

PRICE AND PAYOFF SCHEDULE

MARK ANY 4 NUMBERS			
Catch	Bet 1.00	Bet 2.00	Bet 5.00
2 Wins	1.00	2.00	5.00
3 Wins	3.00	6.00	15.00
4 Wins	125.00	250.00	625.00

MARK ANY 8 NUMBERS			
Catch	Bet 1.00	Bet 2.00	Bet 5.00
5 Wins	9.00	18.00	45.00
6 Wins	90.00	180.00	450.00
7 Wins	1,495.00	2,990.00	7,475.00
8 Wins	25,000.00	50,000.00	50,000.00

A 1-SPOT TICKET wins when the number a player selects is "caught" among the twenty winning numbers the casino draws. Almost all other tickets require more than one catch to win.

Each additional catch increases the size of the payoff. As an example, the $1 4-spot ticket schedule (see the illustration above) requires at least two catches before it can win at all. But the payoff increases further when three or four numbers are caught. The $1 8-spot ticket schedule shown requires at least five catches to win, with the payoff increasing as six, seven, or all eight spots are caught.

WINNING TICKETS are paid by the Keno writers. When a customer presents the duplicate copy of a winning ticket at a Keno window, the writer verifies the amount of the payoff with the supervisor and then pays off the customer. The writer retains the customer's duplicate copy. A federal regulation requires players to present winning tickets for payoff immediately after the game is called. There are always several minutes before another game is called.

MULTIPLE CONSECUTIVE GAMES can be wagered on a single ticket by writing the number of the first game, number of the last game, total number of games, price per game, and total price for all the games in the appropriate boxes. Up to one thousand consecutive games may be played in Nevada casinos. When more than twenty consecutive games are played, all the winnings must be collected within a reasonable amount of time after the last game is called.

TAXES must be paid on net winnings (the payoff minus the price of the ticket) of $1,500 or more. The casino must report the actual net payout, so some casinos permit a player to refuse part of the payoff due if it slightly exceeds $1,500. When a Keno player has a net win exceeding $1,500, the casino will ask the player for his or her social security number and a piece of identification before it pays off. This information is sent to the Internal Revenue Service along with IRS Form W-2G. Players must pay taxes on all their gambling winnings. However, Section 1.165-10 of the Income Tax Code allows gambling losses to be deducted from gambling winnings for income tax purposes (as long as careful records are kept) but not from income derived from any other source besides gambling.

REPLAYING TICKETS from earlier games is offered to players who do not wish to go to the trouble of marking up a new ticket when they play the same spots in the new game.

The player gives the duplicate ticket from a previous game along with the purchase price to a Keno writer, who treats this ticket as if it were the player's original ticket. The Keno writer then issues to the player a duplicate copy of this ticket with the number of the next game printed on it.

KENO RUNNERS are available in many casinos for Keno players who are not in a Keno lounge. A player may ask any employee in the casino or in a dining or drinking facility to call a runner.

Keno runners bring with them blank tickets and black crayons. They take the players' original marked tickets and money and bring them to the Keno writers, who make duplicate copies of the tickets. The runners then return the duplicate tickets and any change due to the players.

As soon as the game is called, the runner makes the rounds with a draw ticket to determine if any of the players are holding winning tickets. The runner takes the duplicate copies of winning tickets to the Keno writers, collects the payoffs, and delivers these to the winning players.

The casino is not responsible if the Keno runner is late and does not get a player's ticket into the current game, although this does not happen very often. In the rare instance when it does happen, the player is given the choice of having the runner either return the wager to him or her or use the ticket to make a wager in the next game.

NEVADA CASINOS set their own payoffs and a maximum aggregate payoff amount, typically $50,000 to $200,000, for all the winning tickets in a given game. On those unusual occasions when the total payoffs for a game exceed the maximum allowed—for example, $200,000—the casino prorates the payoffs so that each winning ticket receives a proportion of the $200,000. For example, if there are two tickets in one game that win $100,000 and a third that wins $50,000, the first two winning tickets would each pay off $80,000 and the latter would pay off $40,000.

THE CASINO ADVANTAGE for the game of Keno is higher than for any other game. It varies slightly for the different types of 1-spot to 15-spot tickets but overall is about 28 percent in Nevada and 49 percent in lottery Keno! But the game is very popular because it offers big prizes for small wagers plus it moves along slowly and is relaxing to play. Thus, the casino advantage percentage for Keno cannot be compared directly to other games. In these, the casino takes a much smaller percentage per decision, but the games go very fast and the wins-per-unit-of-time are higher than the percentage figures indicate because they are calculated on the basis of each decision rather than the length of time it takes to lose a given amount of money.

COMBINATION TICKETS can be created using a single ticket sheet if the spots are divided into separate groups. In the example on the next page, the twelve numbers that have been selected are divided into three groups of four spots each. Three types of standard tickets can be wagered on this single Keno sheet. All spots within a circle must be wagered as a single unit. For instance, all of the spots in circle A must be wagered together. One, two, or even three of the spots cannot be wagered independently of the others in the same group, but the groups can be combined in different ways.

FIRST GAME	NO. OF GAMES	TOTAL PRICE 7.00
LAST GAME		PRICE PER GAME

1	2	3	4	5	6	7	8	9	10
11	12	13	14	15	16	17	18	19	20
21	22	23	24	25	26	27	28	29	30
31	32	33	34	35	36	37	38	39	40

A B

MULTI GAME KENO FROM 2 TO 1000 GAMES IN ADVANCE

41	42	43	44	45	46	47	48	49	50
51	52	53	54	55	56	57	58	59	60
61	62	63	64	65	66	67	68	69	70
71	72	73	74	75	76	77	78	79	80

C

3/IV

3/8

1/12

1.00 Ea

WIN UP TO $200,000 OR MORE

DIFFERENT COMBINATIONS are possible. In the above example, the smallest type of ticket that can be wagered is a standard 4-spot. All of the possible 4-spot tickets must be wagered at the same time because there is no way of indicating that some of the circles are being wagered and not others.

A player who wants to create a 4-spot ticket has to wager on all three circles. This is a 3/4 (3-way 4-spot) ticket. Each of the circles is wagered as an independent standard 4-spot ticket, and each circle is paid off according to the number of catches within it. Circles can be combined with each other, and the circles in the example can be combined into groups of two circles each to create 8-spot tickets. Three 8-spot tickets (A + B, A + C, and B + C) can be created in this example; a player who wants to create 8-spot tickets must wager on all three possible combinations at the same time, as if he or she were using three independent standard 8-spot tickets. This is then called a 3/8 (3-way 8-spot) ticket.

FIRST GAME	NO. OF GAMES	TOTAL PRICE
LAST GAME		7.00
		PRICE PER GAME

X	X	X	X	5	6	7	8	9	10
11	12	13	14	15	16	17	18	19	20
21	22	23	24	25	26	27	28	29	30
31	32	33	X	X	X	X	38	39	40

A (1–4 circled) B (34–37 circled)

MULTI GAME KENO FROM 2 TO 1000 GAMES IN ADVANCE

41	42	43	44	45	46	47	48	49	50
51	52	53	54	55	56	57	58	59	60
61	62	63	64	65	66	67	68	69	70
71	72	73	74	75	76	X	X	X	X

C (77–80 circled)

3/IV

3/8

1/12

1.00 Ea

WIN UP TO $200,000 OR MORE

PLEASE NOTE: This Keno ticket is repeated from the preceding page to make it easier for the reader to follow the text.

ALL THREE OF THE CIRCLES can be combined together (A + B + C) to create a single, standard 12-spot ticket. This is called a 1/12 (1-way 12-spot) ticket.

Only three types of tickets can be wagered on the above Keno sheet: a 3/4 ticket, a 3/8 ticket, and a 1/12 ticket.

A player has the right to wager on any one of these three types of tickets, on any two of them, or on all three of them at the same time. Choices as well as the amount of the wager are written in the right-hand margin of the sheet.

PLAYERS' CHOICES are called "conditions." Players wager only on those types of tickets that they "condition." If the player conditions only one type of ticket, it is called a "way" ticket. If the player conditions more than one type of ticket, it is called a "combination" ticket. The illustration on page 106 shows a combination ticket because it has three different types of tickets conditioned on it.

THE TOTAL PRICE of a ticket is based on the number of ways it has been conditioned, since the player must wager on each condition chosen. In the example, the player is wagering $1 for each conditioned way. The standard 12-spot (1-way 12-spot) ticket is $1. The 3/8 is three standard $1 8-spot tickets that total $3. The 3/4 ticket is three standard $1 4-spot tickets for a total of $3. The example shows a ticket that has been conditioned seven ways:

1 way (12-spot)
3 way (8-spot)
+ 3 way (4-spot)

---

7 ways total

The total price for the ticket is 7 ways times $1, which equals $7, and the total price, $7, is written in the upper right-hand corner of the ticket. In the example, each type of ticket is wagered for $1, so the symbol "1$^{\underline{00}}$ ea" or "1$^{\underline{00}}$ W" (for $1 each way) is written in the lower right corner of the ticket. When different wagers are put on conditioned tickets, they are written as in the illustration on page 109. The price of each type of ticket is placed to the right of the symbol for that ticket. A dash separates the ticket symbol and its price. The minimum price for a standard ticket is usually $1 or $2, but some casinos offer special way-ticket prices that are lower than the minimum—for example, 50¢ on each way—if a minimum number of ways is bet. Not all casinos advertise their special way prices, so always ask what special prices are offered on way and combination tickets.

THE CASINO ADVANTAGE for way and combination tickets is the same as for standard tickets. Wagering on several standard tickets at the same time increases the player's chances of winning, but it also increases the purchase price. The purpose of way and combination tickets is to save players and writers time in marking tickets between games. However, these tickets do create interesting variations with multiple winning possibilities on a single Keno sheet.

CORRECT CONDITIONING is required on way and combination tickets. Players who make a mistake will not be paid the complete payoff on winning tickets. A player's conditions must not allow for more than one interpretation. Otherwise, the casino will be forced to prorate the payoff according to the total number of ways that the player should have wagered the ticket, based on the player's own conditions. However, the problem of an incorrectly conditioned ticket rarely occurs because Keno writers carefully examine way and combination tickets for accuracy before they accept wagers from the players. The player can avoid needless errors by using the following rules to condition way and combination tickets. When the circles on way and combination tickets all contain the same number of spots, the player should calculate the total number of ways the circles can be combined to create a specific type of ticket.

The ticket in the example on page 109 has eight circles, each with three spots. There are five different way tickets that can be conditioned on it:

8-way 3-spot ticket (the individual circles)
28-way 6-spot ticket (groups using two circles)
56-way 9-spot ticket (groups using three circles)
70-way 12-spot ticket (groups using four circles)
56-way 15-spot ticket (groups using five circles)

Tickets cannot be created with more than fifteen spots; therefore, groups of six, seven, or all eight of the circles, each with three spots, cannot be combined together in this example because these groupings would produce tickets with eighteen, twenty-one, and twenty-four spots, respectively. The player can select any one or any combination of the five different types

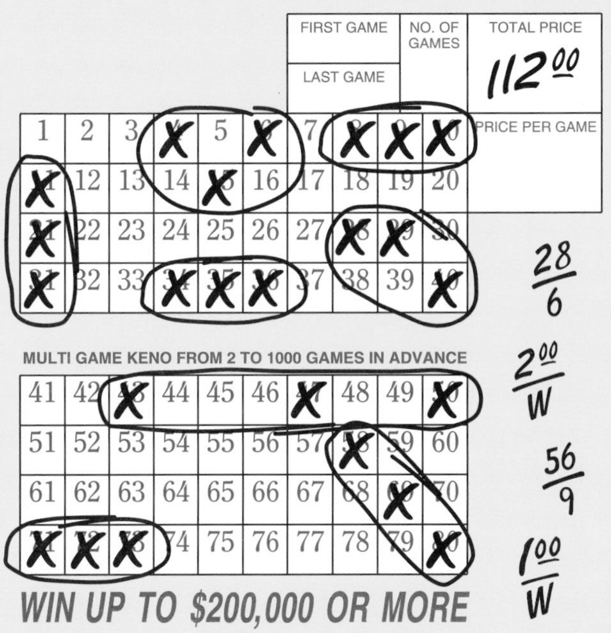

of way tickets shown on page 108 and write the proper conditions in the right-hand margin, but once a player has chosen which types of tickets to wager, he or she must calculate the total number of ways each type of ticket can be wagered. In the example above, the player has selected 6-spot and 9-spot tickets.

To calculate the number of ways each of the above tickets can be created from eight circles, each with three spots, you first create a fraction. Here is how to proceed. Note that the numerator refers to the numerals on top of the fraction; the denominator refers to the numerals below the line (for example, $\frac{\text{numerator}}{\text{denominator}}$).

1) The denominator always begins with the numeral on the left and increases in the following progression: 1 x 2 x 3 x 4, etc. The number of numerals in the denominator is always equal to the number of circles (never the number of spots) that are being combined to increase the specific type of ticket.

28-way 6-spot (using two circles)

$$\frac{}{1 \times 2} =$$

56-way 9-spot (using three circles)

$$\frac{}{1 \times 2 \times 3} =$$

2) The numerator always begins with the total number of circles (never the number of spots) that have been marked on the ticket and decreases in the following progression: 8 x 7 x 6 x 5, etc. Note that the number of numerals in the numerator is always equal to the number of numerals in the denominator.

28-way 6-spot (using two circles)

$$\frac{8 \times 7}{1 \times 2} =$$

56-way 9-spot (using three circles)

$$\frac{8 \times 7 \times 6}{1 \times 2 \times 3} =$$

3) The numerator and denominator are then canceled and multiplied out.

28-way 6-spot (using two circles)

$$\frac{4 \times 7}{1 \times 1} = 28$$

56-way 9-spot (using three circles)

$$\frac{4 \times 7 \times 2}{1 \times 1 \times 1} = 56$$

The result is the total number of ways that the circles can be combined to produce the specific type of ticket. The number of ways each type of ticket can be conditioned is written in the right margin: 28/6 (28-way 6-spot) and 56/9 (56-way 9-spot).

4) The price for each type of ticket is multiplied by the number of ways that the ticket can be created: $2 x 28 ways = $56 and $1 x 56 = $56. Then the prices for each conditioned ticket are added together to obtain the total price for the ticket: $56 + $56 = $112.

As shown on page 112, some circles contain five spots, others contain four, and the rest contain three spots. When the circles on way and combination tickets contain a different number of spots, the following formula is used to calculate the total number of ways the circles can be combined to create the specific type of ticket: All the circles containing a certain number of spots are multiplied by all the circles containing another number of spots.

For example, 8-spot tickets can be created by combining each 3-spot circle with each 5-spot circle. Three circles contain five spots, and four circles contain three spots, so 3 x 4 = 12 ways.

One other 8-spot ticket can be created by combining the two circles that contain four spots. Every combination of the number of spots selected must be wagered, in this case thirteen ways to create eight spots.

Groups of four spots or less should be enclosed within circles, and groups of five spots or more should be enclosed within lines, as this ticket shows. However, there are situations in which groups of five or more numbers must be circled for clarity.

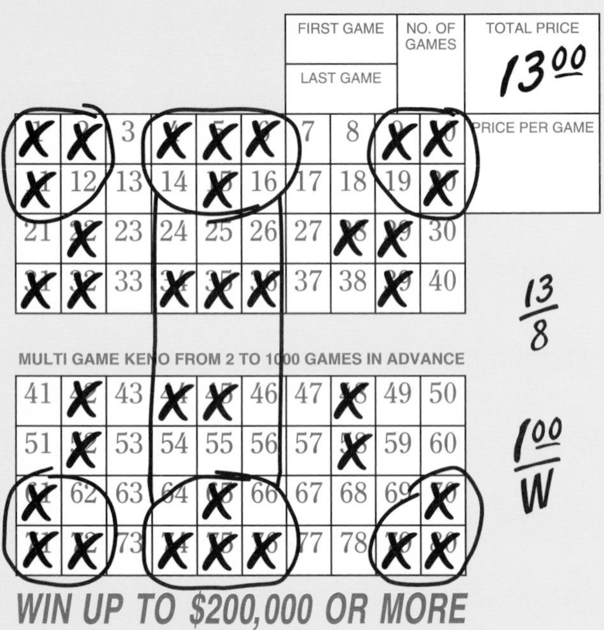

A WAY TICKET PAYOFF is calculated after the number of catches in each circle is determined. Keno writers mark the catches with long slashes, as shown on the ticket on page 113. This is a way ticket because there is only one condition in the right-hand margin. If it were a combination ticket with more than one condition, each type of condition would be evaluated individually using the following method for way tickets, and the payoffs for each of the conditions would be added together to obtain the total payoff.

The easiest and most accurate method to calculate the payoff for a way ticket is shown in the table found on page 114. First, a fraction is created. The number of numerals that appear in both the numerator and in the denominator is equal to the number of circles. The numerals in the numerator represent the number of spots in each circle, for example the three spots in each of the five circles. The numerals in the denominator represent the number of catches in each circle.

DATE	TIME	RATE	MULTI	TOTAL PRICE
Dec 23, 1995	8:38 PM	1.00		$10.00

REPLAY #	ACCOUNT #	1st GAME	LAST	WRITER	SERIAL #
		742		50	2-12810

1	2 A	3	4	5	6	7	8	9 B	10
11	12 A	13	14	15	16	17	18 B	19 B	20
21	22 A	23	24	25	26 C	27	28	29	30
31	32	33	34	35 C	36 C	37	38	39	40

10/9 1.00

PER GAME 10.00

PAID 3

MULTI GAME KENO FROM 2 TO 1000 GAMES IN ADVANCE

41	42	43	44	45	46	47	48	49	50
51	52	53	54 D	55	56	57	58	59 E	60
61	62	63	64 D	65	66	67	68	69	70 E
71	72	73	74 D	75	76	77	78	79 E	80

WEST GAME

4,440.00

A step-by-step analysis is made of every possible payoff. It begins with the largest number of catches and continues down to the least number of catches. The only reason that the 2-1-0 catch is included (three catches on a standard 9-spot ticket do not win any payoff) is to list every possible combination. The total number of combinations of catches is always equal to the total number of ways that have been conditioned. In this example there are ten possible conditioned ways and ten combinations of catches. When customers calculate every possible combination of catches, they ensure that they don't miss any combination that might win a payoff.

$$\frac{\text{(Circles) } 3\text{-}3\text{-}3\text{-}3\text{-}3}{\text{(Catches) } 3\text{-}3\text{-}2\text{-}1\text{-}0} = \text{10 way 9-spot}$$

1)	3-3-2	1/8	$4,000.00
2)	3-3-1	1/7	300.00
3)	3-3-0	1/6	44.00
4)	3-2-1	1/6	44.00
5)	3-2-1	1/6	44.00
6)	3-2-0	1/5	4.00
7)	3-2-0	1/5	4.00
8)	3-1-0	1/4	.00
9)	3-1-0	1/4	.00
10)	2-1-0	1/3 +	.00

TOTAL PAYOFF = $4,440.00

PRICE AND PAYOFF SCHEDULE

MARK ANY 9 NUMBERS			
Catch	**Bet 1.00**	**Bet 2.00**	**Bet 5.00**
5 Wins	4.00	8.00	20.00
6 Wins	44.00	88.00	220.00
7 Wins	300.00	600.00	1,500.00
8 Wins	4,000.00	8,000.00	20,000.00
9 Wins	25,000.00	Progressive	Progressive

DATE	TIME	RATE	MULTI	TOTAL PRICE
Dec 23, 1995	8:38 PM	1.00		$10.00

REPLAY #	ACCOUNT #	1st GAME	LAST	WRITER	SERIAL #
		742		50	2-12810

1	2 A	3	4	5	6	7	8	9 B	10
11	12 A	13	14	15	16	17	18 B	19 B	20
21	22 A	23	24	25	26 C	27	28	29	30
31	32	33	34	35 C	36 C	37	38	39	40

10/9 1.00

PER GAME 10.00

PAID 3

MULTI GAME KENO FROM 2 TO 1000 GAMES IN ADVANCE

41	42	43	44	45	46	47	48	49	50
51	52	53	54 D	55	56	57	58	59 E	60
61	62	63	64 D	65	66	67	68	69	70 E
71	72	73	74 D	75	76	77	78	79 E	80

WEST GAME

4,440.00

FIRST GAME	NO. OF GAMES	TOTAL PRICE
LAST GAME		2.00

1	2	3	4	5	6	7	X	9	10
11	12	13	14	15	16	X	18	19	20
21	22	23	X	X	26	27	28	29	30
X	32	33	34	35	36	37	38	(X)	40

PRICE PER GAME

1/8

MULTI GAME KENO FROM 2 TO 1000 GAMES IN ADVANCE

41	42	43	44	45	46	47	48	49	50
X	52	53	54	55	56	X	58	59	60
61	62	63	64	65	66	67	68	X	70
71	72	73	74	75	76	77	78	79	80

1/9

1.00 / Ea

WIN UP TO $200,000 OR MORE

A KING TICKET has circles that contain only one spot. A King circle is treated just like any other circle, but it is given special acknowledgment because any standard ticket can be converted easily into a combination ticket by simply circling only one spot. In the example above, the standard 9-spot ticket is also a standard 8-spot ticket. The simplest way to create a combination ticket is to circle one spot, and it is the easiest combination ticket in which to calculate the payoff because there are just two obvious conditions.

FIRST GAME	NO. OF GAMES	TOTAL PRICE 31.00
LAST GAME		PRICE PER GAME

1	2	3	4	5	6	7	8	9	10
11	12	13	14	15	16	17	18	19	20
21	22	23	24	25	26	27	28	29	30
31	32	33	34	35	36	37	38	39	40

MULTI GAME KENO FROM 2 TO 1000 GAMES IN ADVANCE

41	42	43	44	45	46	47	48	49	50
51	52	53	54	55	56	57	58	59	60
61	62	63	64	65	66	67	68	69	70
71	72	73	74	75	76	77	78	79	80

5/ONE
10/TWO
10/III
5/IV
1/V
1.00/Ea

WIN UP TO $200,000 OR MORE

In the unusual example above right, all five spots are circled as King spots. Each circle can be combined with every other circle to create 2- through 5-spot tickets. Every possible combination in this example has been conditioned. This illustration contains the symbols used by most casinos to condition 1- through 5-spot tickets. The words "one" and "two" are written out for 1-spot and 2-spot tickets. Roman numerals are used to denote 3-spot, 4-spot, and 5-spot tickets, and Arabic numerals are used to identify 6- to 15-spot tickets.

PLAYERS
BANKERS
BANKERS
BANKERS
PLAYERS
PLAYERS
2
3
4
5
6

BACCARAT

Baccarat (pronounced BAH-kah-rah) games are usually partitioned off by a rail from the rest of the gaming area. This affords a certain degree of privacy to the players, who may have large amounts of chips sitting on the table.

Two hands are dealt in the game of Baccarat; every player has the option of wagering on either hand. Two or three cards are dealt to each hand; the hand with the point total closest to 9 wins.

Left: Baccarat in action. Above: Mini-Baccarat being played.

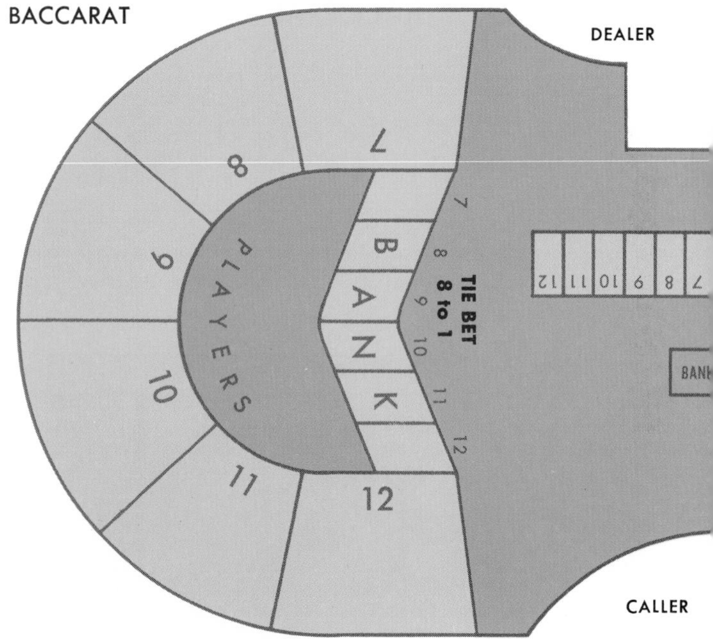

SEAT NUMBERS are placed in front of every chair in order to make it easy to identify each player's hands and wagers. The seats are numbered 1 through 12. If there are more than 12 seats, the numbers usually continue with 14, the number 13 being eliminated to accommodate any superstitious beliefs on the parts of those players who consider it unlucky.

Beyond the number at each seat is a space for the Player Hand Bet, the Bank Hand Bet, and the Tie Bet toward the center of the table. The numbers on the Bank Hand Bet boxes and the Commission Marker boxes correspond to the respective seat numbers.

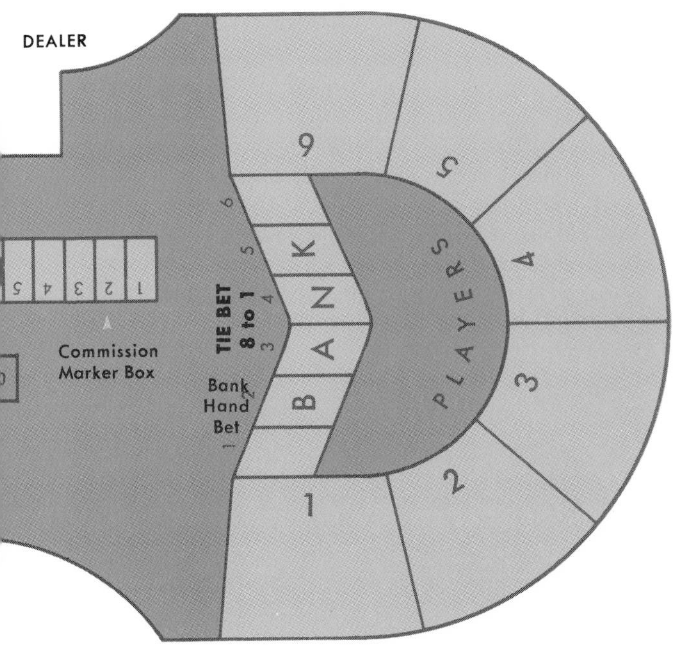

Three employees, two dealers and a caller, are used to operate each Baccarat game. The two dealers, who stand along one side in the center of the table, are responsible for the wagers on their respective sides. They collect all the losing wagers and pay the winning wagers. They also record, in the row of Commission Marker boxes in front of them, the money each player owes to the casino in Commissions.

Standing across from the two dealers is the caller, who directs the game. This person also tells the players when to deal the cards and makes an announcement of the winning hand.

THE TWO HANDS dealt in each game of Baccarat are called the "Bank Hand" and the "Player Hand." These names are arbitrary and mean, basically, "Hand Number 1" and "Hand Number 2." The player has the option of wagering on either hand and may switch from one hand to the other on successive deals.

BANK HAND WAGERS are placed in the boxes that are collectively labeled BANK, which are highlighted in the illustration below. Players use the Bank Hand box that is directly behind their seat number.

Bank Hand Bet

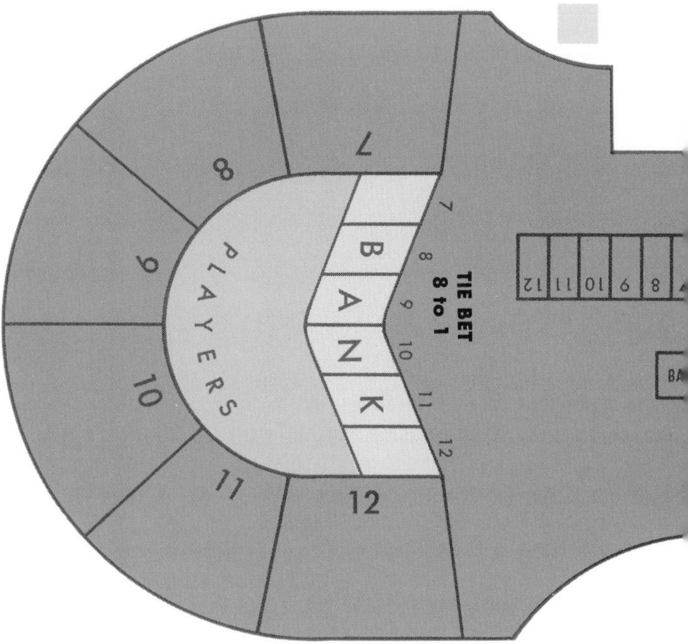
7
8
9
10
11
12
PLAYERS
BANK
7
8
9
10
11
12
TIE BET
8 to 1
12
11
10
9
8

PLAYER HAND WAGERS are placed in the areas that are highlighted with the word PLAYERS, as seen in the illustration below. Some casinos do not divide the Player Hand Bet areas into individual boxes. In these casinos players set their wagers just across the line from their seat number space in the Player Hand area, with the money—if they are playing with cash—pointing toward them. In some casinos only chips are allowed to be wagered, no cash. Nevada casinos used to pay off winnings with cash, but no casino does this today.

Player Hand Bet

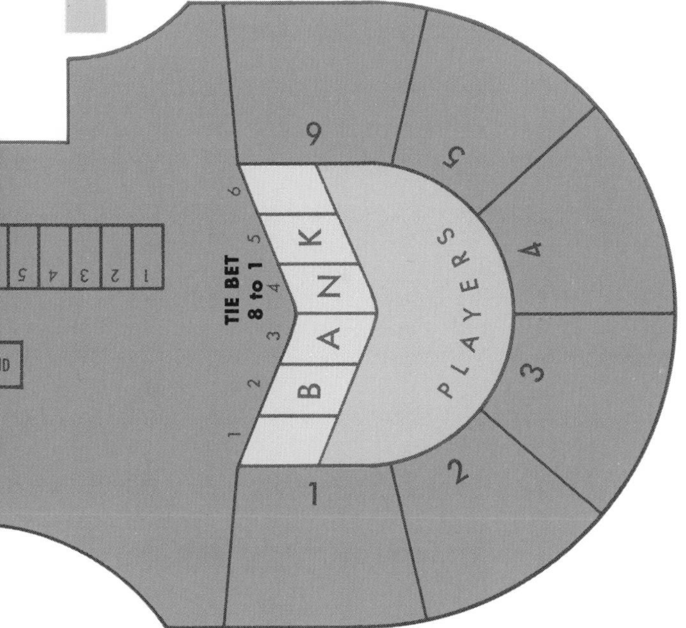

CARD VALUES—10's and the picture cards—Jacks, Queens, and Kings—equal 0. Aces equal 1. The rest of the cards are equal to their face value. The four suits (Spades, Hearts, Diamonds, and Clubs) have no meaning in Baccarat.

HAND VALUES

Only numerals in red count

2 + 3 = 5 2 + 1 + 4 = 7

0 + 9 = 9 0 + 3 + 7 = 10

8 + 9 = 17 8 + 3 + 5 = 16

HAND VALUES—When the values of the two or three cards in a single hand are added together, only the number that is on the right-hand side of the final figure is to be counted. This number by itself is considered the point total for the hand. As an example, 8 + 9 = 17. Since in this card game only the 7 counts, the hand equals 7.

The only possible point totals in the game of Baccarat are the numbers 0 through 9 (0, 1, 2, 3, 4, 5, 6, 7, 8, and 9). The hand that has the point total that is the closest to 9 wins.

The dealers shuffle together the eight standard 52-card decks that are used to play the game of Baccarat. A cut card with a different colored back is inserted near the end of the combined decks. These decks are then placed in a dealing box called a shoe.

CARD VALUES

EACH CARD = FACE VALUE

EACH CARD = FACE VALUE

EACH CARD = 0

AN ACE = 1

THE BURN CARDS are removed from the shoe and put into the "discard" bowl in the center of the table. To determine the number of burn cards, the caller removes the first card from the shoe and turns it face up. The point value of this card (in this case, picture cards are worth 10 points) dictates the number of cards that are to be burned. In the illustration below, the first card removed from the shoe is a 3, so the caller burns three more cards before he or she directs the first hand to be dealt to the players.

Cards from completed hands are also placed in the discard bowl by the caller. When the shuffled cards are

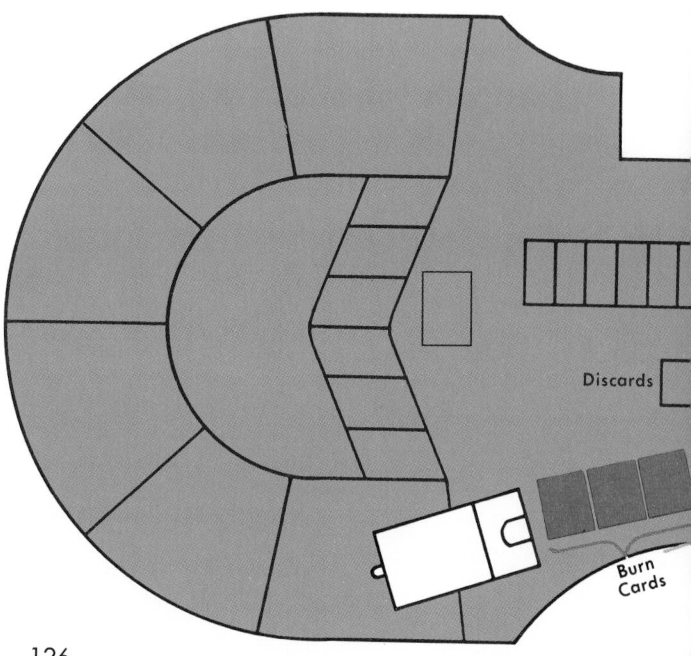

almost depleted, the cut card reaches the window in the front of the shoe. If it appears while a hand is in progress, that hand and one more hand after it are completed. If the cut card appears between hands, then two additional hands are dealt before the cards are reshuffled. Casinos that offer high maximum limits will usually take out new decks of cards and shuffle them instead of shuffling the used cards, which are removed. The casino is permitted to reshuffle the cards after the completion of any hand, even if the cut card has not yet appeared; however, no reshuffling may take place once a hand is in progress.

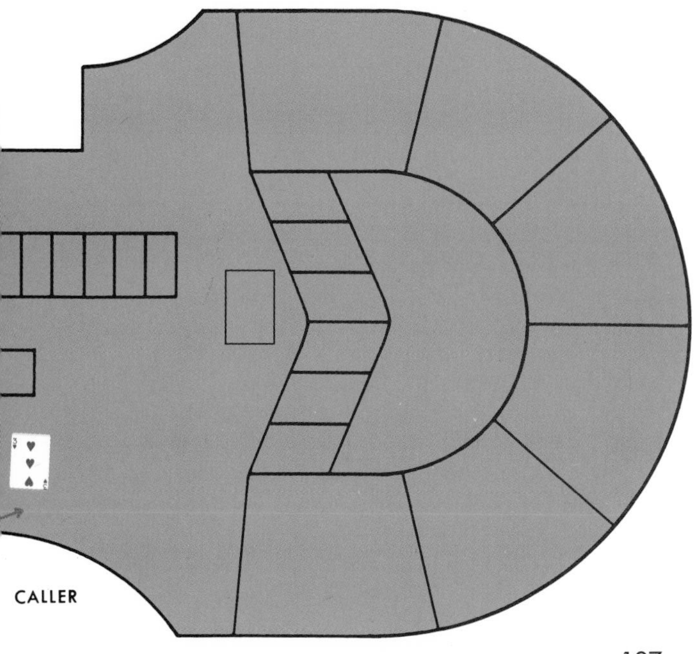

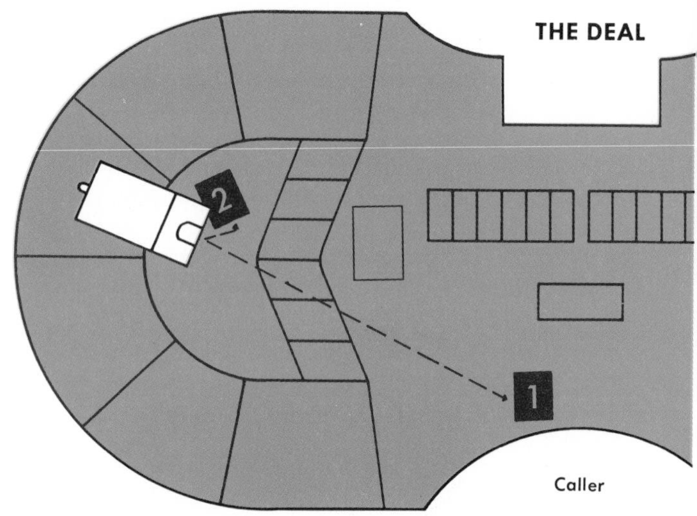

DEALING BY PLAYERS is optional. No player is forced to deal the cards. On being given the shoe, the player can merely pass it on to the player on his or her right. But most players like to hold the shoe and deal.

The player who is dealing must wager at least the table minimum on either the Bank Hand Bet or the Player Hand Bet before dealing the cards, but he or she may switch the wager from one bet to the other after the hand is completed. That same player may continue to deal as long as the Bank Hand does not lose, but as soon as the Player Hand Bet wins, the player must pass the shoe to the player who is sitting on his or her right. This person now has the option of dealing the cards or passing the shoe. The shoe always travels in a counter-clockwise motion.

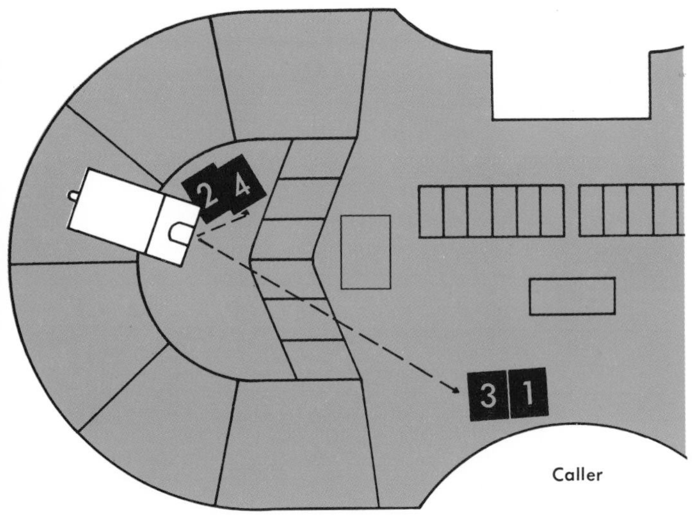

THE CALLER supervises the deal after all the players have wagered on either the Bank Hand Bet or the Player Hand Bet. Players never deal until instructed by the caller, who will answer any questions for an inexperienced player. The caller's instruction, "Cards, please," directs the player to deal two cards, face down, to each hand.

The player slides the first card, which is for the Player Hand, to the caller, then tucks the second card, which is for the Bank Hand, under the front corner of the shoe that is farthest away from the caller so that it will not be in the way when the remaining cards are dealt. Finally, the player slides the third card to the caller and tucks the fourth card under the previous Bank Hand card.

A FACED HAND is a hand where the cards are turned face up after they have been dealt, all under the direction of the caller. The caller gives the two Player Hand cards, which are held face down, to a player who has a wager on the Player Hand Bet. This is usually the player with the biggest Player Hand wager. This player immediately turns the cards face up and then tosses them back to the caller. The caller announces the point total for the two cards and lays them down in front of him or her in the Player Hand card area.

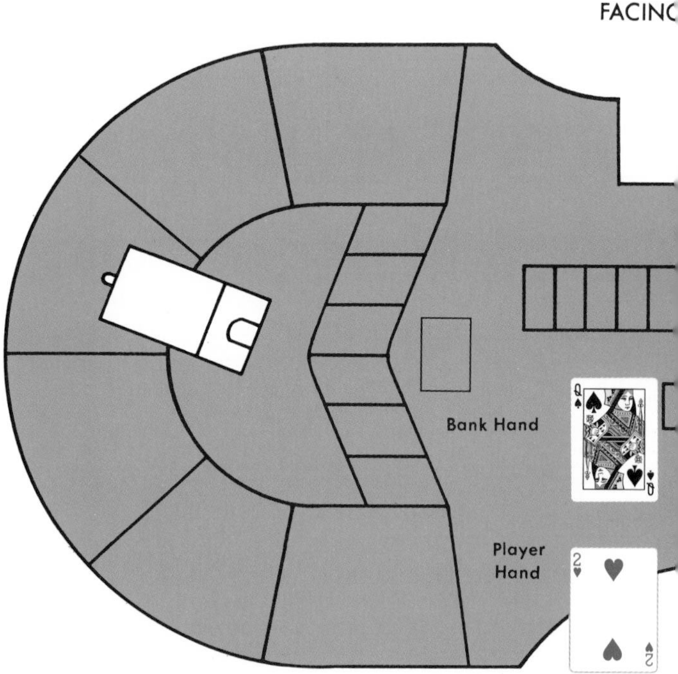

If none of the players have made a Player Hand wager, the caller faces the Player Hand cards. Then he or she lays them down in the Player Hand area.

After the Player Hand cards are laid down on the table, the player who dealt the hand removes the two Bank Hand cards from under the corner of the shoe and faces the cards. Then he or she tosses them over to the caller. At this point the caller announces the point total for the two cards and lays them down in the Bank Hand card area.

THE HANDS

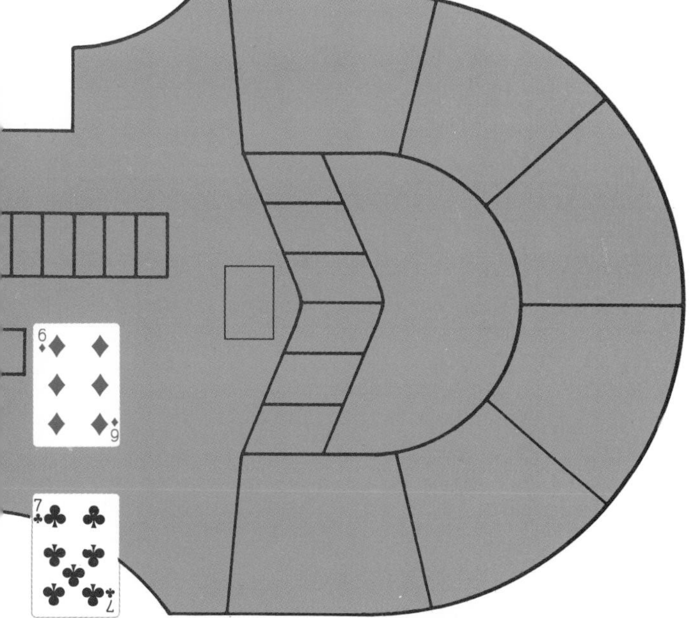

NATURAL HANDS

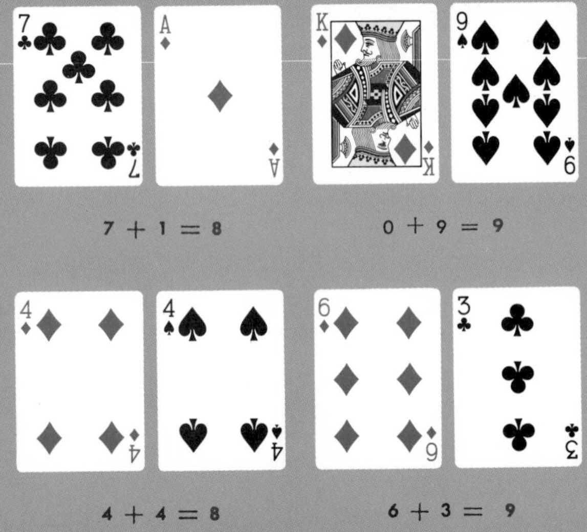

Only numerals in red count

A NATURAL HAND is a hand that is made up of two cards that total either 8 or 9. When either the Bank Hand or the Player Hand is dealt a Natural 8 or a Natural 9, the game is over. Neither hand may draw a third card. As soon as the cards are faced, the caller declares the hand that has the highest point total the winner. Natural 9 is the best hand. It wins over a Natural 8.

TIE HANDS

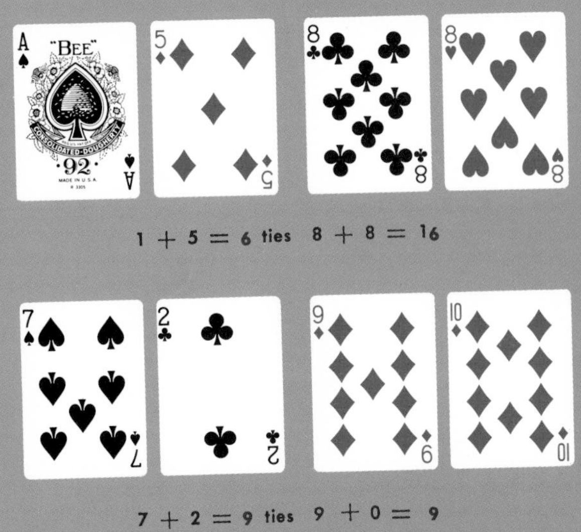

A TIE HAND occurs when both the Bank Hand and the Player Hand have the same point total at the conclusion of the deal. A tie hand is often referred to as a push, draw, or standoff. When there is a tie, the wagers are neither won nor lost. They belong once again to the players, who have the choice of wagering again on either of the two hands, increasing or decreasing the sizes of their wagers, or quitting.

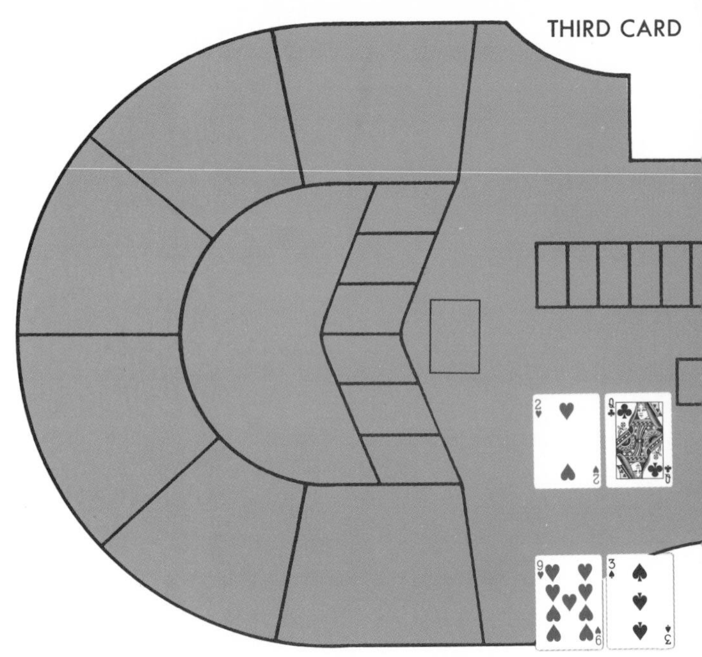

"Bank wins, 7 over 3."

THE THIRD CARD is the final card that can be dealt to either hand. Third-card rules apply in every single situation and dictate whether or not a third card is dealt. Most players deal the cards without knowing the third-card rules because the caller always directs the action, using a fixed set of rules. As an example, the player who has the shoe does not deal a third card until the caller requests it. Then the player always deals this card face up to the caller, who lays it down next to the initial two cards while announcing the new point total for the hand.

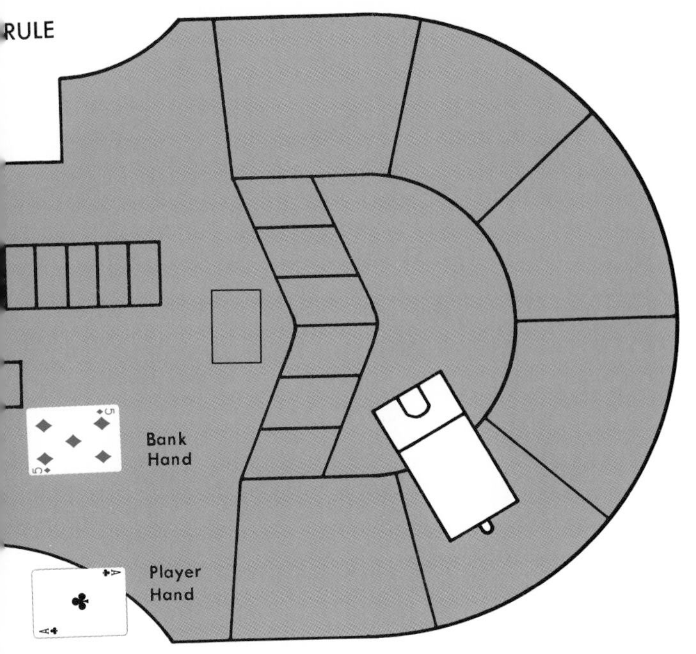

When third-card rules call for the Player Hand to stand on the initial two cards, the caller states, "Player stands with (point total)." When the rules require a third card for the Player Hand, the caller requests a "card for the Player." After the Player Hand is concluded, the Bank Hand is completed in the same fashion. When both hands are complete, the caller declares the hand with the highest point total the winner. For example, "Bank wins, 7 over 3," or "Player wins, 1 over 0," or, in the case of a tie, "Tie hand, 6 to 6; nobody wins."

PLAYER HAND THIRD CARD RULES

0 to 5 — Player Hand must draw
6 and 7 — Player Hand must stand
8 and 9 — Natural — both stand

THE PLAYER HAND MUST STAND IF THE POINT TOTAL OF THE INITIAL TWO CARDS IS 6 OR MORE (6, 7, 8, OR 9) AND MUST DRAW IF THE POINT TOTAL OF THE INITIAL TWO CARDS IS 5 OR LESS (1, 2, 3, 4, OR 5).

WHEN THE PLAYER HAND STANDS because it has a point total of 6 or 7 on the initial two cards, the third-card rules for the Bank Hand are identical to the Player Hand third-card rules stated at the top of this page. So when the Player Hand stands with 6 or 7, the Bank Hand must also stand with a point total of 6 or 7 on the initial two cards, but the Bank Hand must draw a third card with a point total of 5 or less.

WHEN THE PLAYER HAND DRAWS a third card because it has a point total of 5 or less on the initial two cards, and the Bank Hand has a point total of 3 to 6 on the initial two cards, the third-card rules for the Bank Hand are different from the Player Hand third-card rules. The third-card rules that govern the Bank Hand are determined by the point value of the third card drawn by the Player Hand.

BANK HAND THIRD CARD RULES

WHEN PLAYER HAND DRAWS

0 to 2 — Bank Hand must draw
3 to 6 — Third card to Player Hand determines if draw or stand
7 — Bank Hand must stand
8 and 9 — Natural — both hands stand

THE BANK HAND MUST STAND IF THE POINT TOTAL OF THE INITIAL TWO CARDS IS 7 OR MORE (7, 8, OR 9) AND MUST DRAW IF THE POINT TOTAL OF THE INITIAL TWO CARDS IS 2 OR LESS (0, 1, OR 2).

THIRD CARD RULES
WHEN BANK HAND TOTALS 3 to 6

Bank Hand Total	Bank Hand DRAWS if Player Hand Drew	Bank Hand STANDS if Player Hand Drew
3	1-2-3-4-5-6-7 9-10	8
4	2-3-4-5-6-7	1 8-9-10
5	4-5-6-7	1-2-3 8-9-10
6	6-7	1-2-3-4-5 8-9-10

WHEN THE BANK HAND POINT TOTAL is 3 to 6 on the initial two cards and the Player Hand has drawn a third card, the point value of the third card drawn by the Player Hand determines whether the Bank Hand stands or draws. Bank Hand third-card rules are presented in the diagram above. In the two sections of the diagram, "Bank Hand Draws" and "Bank Hand Stands" are seen to be exact opposites because the point value of the third card drawn by the Player Hand requires that the Bank Hand draw a third card (see left-hand side of diagram) or stand on the initial two cards (see right-hand side of diagram).

These third-card rules create a unique gaming situation. Even when the initial two-card point total for the Bank Hand is greater than the three-card point total for the Player Hand, the Bank Hand may still be forced to draw a third card, which may reduce its point total. The decision to draw a third card in these situations is determined solely by the point value of the third card drawn by the Player Hand, not the needs of the Bank Hand.

For example, if the Bank Hand has a point total of 4 on its initial two cards and if the Player Hand has a point total of only 3 after drawing a 2 for its third card, the Bank Hand still must draw a third card. In this case, the Bank Hand will reduce its point total and lose if it draws a 6, 7, or 8 and tie if it draws a 9.

WAGERING LIMITS	PAYOFFS
Minimum $5, $20, or $25	Player Hand 1 to 1
Maximum $500 to $15,000	Bank Hand 1 to 1, minus 5% Commission

MINI-BACCARAT is played using a table similar in size to the one used for Blackjack, and there is only one dealer. The rules are the same as those for regular Baccarat, but the dealer runs the game alone. The players never touch the shoe or the cards, and the wagering limits are lower.

WAGERING LIMITS are higher for Baccarat than for other casino games. The typical minimum wager for Baccarat is $20 or $25; Mini-Baccarat often has a $5 minimum. The typical maximum wager for Mini-Baccarat is $500 and for the regular game is usually between $5,000 and $15,000. Players lay their chips or cash in the numbered spaces in front of their chairs.

PLAYER HAND PAYOFFS are always in the ratio of 1 to 1—for example, a $5 payoff for every $5 wager, a $20 payoff for every $20 wager, etc. The casino has an advantage because the Player Hand loses more often than it wins, due to the differences in the third-card rules for the Player Hand and the Bank Hand.

BANK HAND PAYOFFS are also in the ratio of 1 to 1. Since the Bank Hand wins more often than it loses, the casino creates an advantage by charging a 5 percent Commission on all winning Bank Hand payoffs. The dealers pay off $5 for every $5 wager, $20 for every $20 wager, etc., but winners of Bank Hand wagers must give the casino 5 percent of the payoff. In reality the player wins only $19 for every $20 bet on the Bank

Hand. However, the dealers pay off 1 to 1—e.g., $20 to $20—and tally up the Commission fees separately to simplify each payoff and speed up the game.

Baccarat is derived from the French game of Chemin de Fer, in which one player is the Bank and all the rest can wager only on the Player Hand. The rules are similar, but the game of Chemin de Fer requires two or more players, with at least one having a large bankroll to "fade" everyone else's Player Hand wagers.

COMMISSION MARKERS are used to record the Commission obligations of players. Every time a dealer pays off a winning Bank Hand wager at the ratio of 1 to 1, a Commission Marker equal to 5 percent of the payoff—25¢ on a $5 payoff, $1 on a $20 payoff, $5 on a $100 payoff, etc.—is placed in the Commission Marker box containing each player's seat number. Every time a player wins a Bank Hand wager, 5 percent of the payoff is added to the total amount in the Commission Marker box for that player.

Players must pay their Commission fees to the casino on demand. Dealers usually ask players to pay their Commission obligation every time the combined decks of cards are shuffled, and all players must pay their Commission Markers before leaving the table.

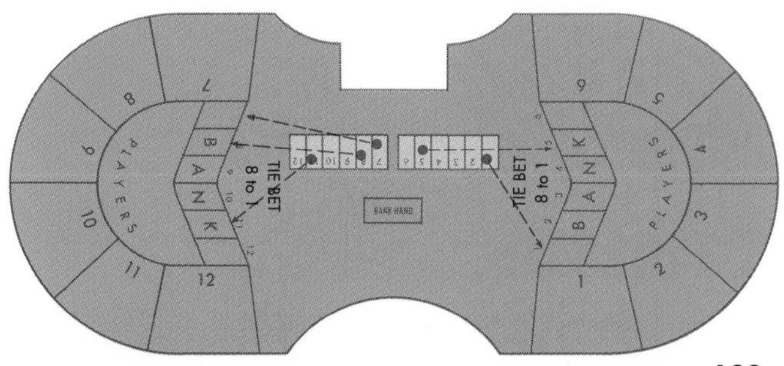

THE CASINO ADVANTAGE for the Bank Hand Bet and Player Hand Bet is about the same. The casino advantage is obtained with the Player Hand Bet because players lose more often than they win. The casino advantage is earned with the Bank Hand Bet, even though players win more often than they lose, because the casino deducts a 5 percent Commission from the payoff—pays off only 95¢ for every $1 wagered.

The Bank Hand has a slightly lower casino advantage, because even with the Commission, the Bank Hand wins often enough to make it a better bet than the Player Hand. There is much discussion as to the exact casino advantage with these two bets. In his book *The Theory of Gambling and Statistical Logic,* Richard A. Bernstein lists the Bank Hand casino advantage at 1.16 percent and the Player Hand at 1.37 percent. These two bets have the lowest casino advantage except for the Odds Bets in Craps, when added to the Pass, Come, Don't Pass, and Don't Come Bets.

THE TIE HAND BET is a Proposition Bet offered in the game of Baccarat. Players place this wager in the appropriate location in front of them. On the next deal, this bet wins if both the Bank Hand and the Player Hand end up with the same total and loses if the two hands have different totals. When this bet wins, the dealer pays the player eight times the wager and leaves the original wager in place for the next deal. After winning, the player may take back the original wager. A winning Tie wager is paid off 8 to 1, and the casino advantage is 13.96 percent. A few casinos have paid 9 to 1 for winning Tie wagers, lowering the casino advantage to 4.4 percent, but this is still a bigger disadvantage for the player than the Bank Hand and Player Hand bets.

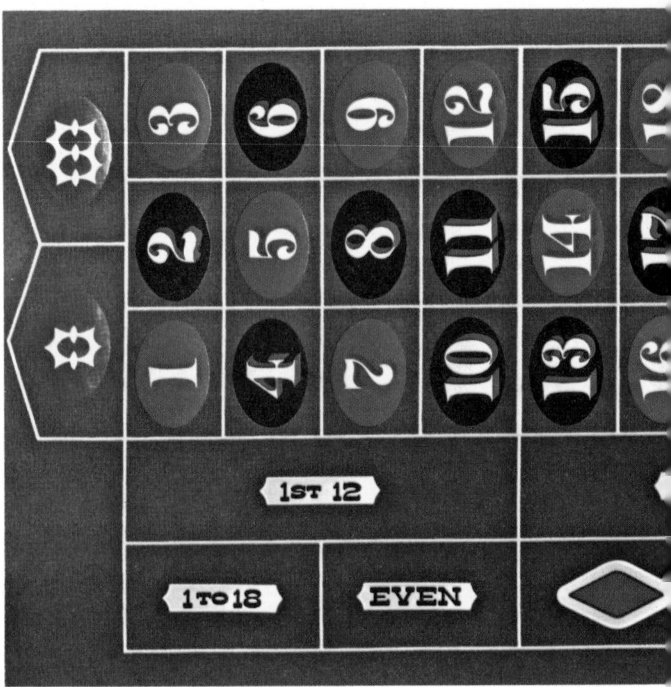

At the Roulette table, a player may wager on one, two, three, four, five, six, twelve, or eighteen numbers at one time. If the player's wager is on

THE ROULETTE TABLE that is in general use throughout the United States has a wheel with thirty-eight numbered metal pockets (1 to 36 plus 0 and 00) in which the rotating ball may land. There is also a layout with the same numbers printed on it. Eighteen of the numbers are in red, eighteen are in black, and 0 and 00 are in green.

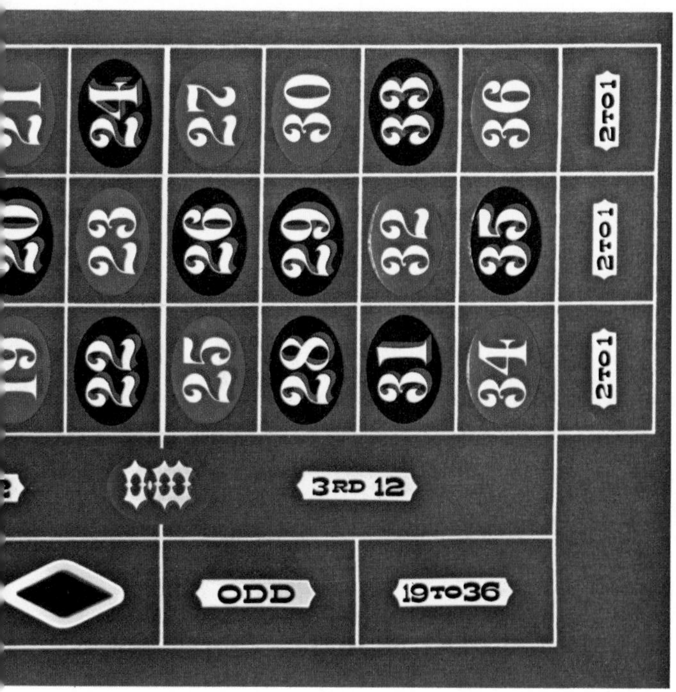

the same number as the one on which the ball lands on the Roulette wheel, the player wins; otherwise, the wager is lost.

The player should be sure that each chip is carefully placed on the chosen bet since each spin of the ball results in every wager being either won or lost. If a player cannot personally reach a certain number or area, he or she can slide the wager toward the dealer and tell him or her what number or combination of numbers to place the wager on.

WAGERS may be made with regular casino chips or Roulette chips. In some jurisdictions, currency may be played on the outside bets. Roulette chips have no monetary value printed on them and can be purchased from the dealer at the table with either currency or regular casino chips.

Each player receives a set of Roulette chips in a different color. Since there is only one place on the Roulette layout to make each bet, owners of winning chips can then be identified by their chip color. When more than one player wants to bet on the same number, the chips are piled on top of one another.

Players declare the value of their chips when purchasing them. This may be any amount between the table minimum and the table maximum.

The dealer places in the Value Indicator a colored chip plus a numbered marker button to indicate the value of the chips. The numbered marker may be put on top of the colored chip on the rim of the wheel. The number on the button represents twenty of the chips, so a colored chip marked with the number 20, for example, means that those colored chips are worth $1 each. If the value of the chip is equal to the table minimum, no marker may be used at all.

ROULETTE CHIPS are purchased in quantities of twenty, called "stacks." Before leaving the table, the player must cash in any leftover Roulette chips, because they cannot be used or even exchanged for regular chips anywhere else in the casino.

COST OF CHIPS

Stack of chips		Chip value		Purchase price
20 chips	x	$ .25	=	$5.00
20 chips	x	$ .50	=	$10.00
20 chips	x	$1.00	=	$20.00

ON THE INSIDE of the layout the player may wager on anywhere from one to six numbers by placing chips directly on the numbers and the lower borderline.

ON THE OUTSIDE of the layout the player may wager on twelve or eighteen numbers. Chips for these bets are placed in any of the twelve larger betting boxes.

INSIDE

00	3	6	9	12	15	18	21	24	27	30	33	36	2to1
	2	5	8	11	14	17	20	23	26	29	32	35	2to1
0	1	4	7	10	13	16	19	22	25	28	31	34	2to1
	1st 12				2nd 12				3rd 12				
	1 to 18		EVEN		RED		BLACK		ODD		19to36		

OUTSIDE

1 NUMBER BET PAYS 35 TO 1

00	3	6	9	12	15	18	21	24	27	30	33	36	2to1
	2	5	8	11	14 ●	17	20	23	26	29	32	35	2to1
0	1	4	7	10	13	16	19	22	25	28	31	34	2to1
	1st 12				2nd 12				3rd 12				
	1 to 18		EVEN		RED		BLACK		ODD		19to36		

WHEN A CHIP IS CENTERED on the single winning number, the player is paid 35 to 1. Each wager wins or loses, depending on the result of the next spin of the wheel. As long as the wager covers the number on which the ball lands, it wins. Each of the red and black numbers and green 0 and 00 may be wagered on individually. The numbers 0 and 00 are treated exactly the way the other numbers are treated. They win and lose in the same fashion and pay the same odds.

38 WAYS TO BET 1 NUMBER
2 INVOLVE 0 AND 00

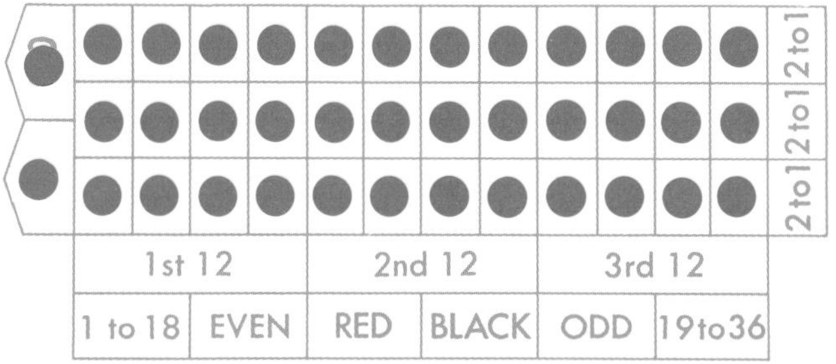

A SPLIT BET is a two-number bet that may be made by placing a chip across any line that separates two numbers. If the ball lands on either one of the two numbers, the bet pays off 17 to 1.

2 NUMBER BET PAYS 17 TO 1

00	3	6	9	12	15	18	21	24	27	30	33	36	2to1
	2	5	8	11	14	17	20	23	26	29	32	35	2to1
0	1	4	7	10	13	16	19	22	25	28	31	34	2to1
	1st 12				2nd 12				3rd 12				
	1 to 18		EVEN		RED		BLACK		ODD		19to36		

THERE IS ONLY ONE BET that can be made at two different locations on the Roulette layout. This Split Bet is made on the line that separates the two green numbers or on the "Courtesy Line," which is between the 2nd Dozen and 3rd Dozen bets on the outside of the Roulette layout. Most casinos do not have the Split Bet printed on the outside of the layout, but it is accepted in just about all casinos.

63 WAYS TO BET 2 NUMBERS
6 INVOLVE 0 AND 00

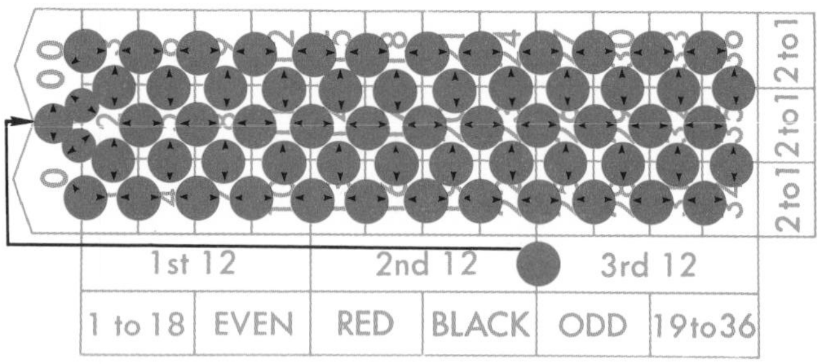

3 NUMBER BET PAYS 11 TO 1

00	3	6	9	12	15	18	21	24	27	30	33	36	2to1
	2	5	8	11	14	17	20	23	26	29	32	35	2to1
0	1	4	7	10	13	16	19	22	25	28	31	34	2to1
	1st 12				2nd 12				3rd 12			
	1 to 18		EVEN		RED		BLACK		ODD		19to36	

15 WAYS TO BET 3 NUMBERS
3 INVOLVE 0 AND 00

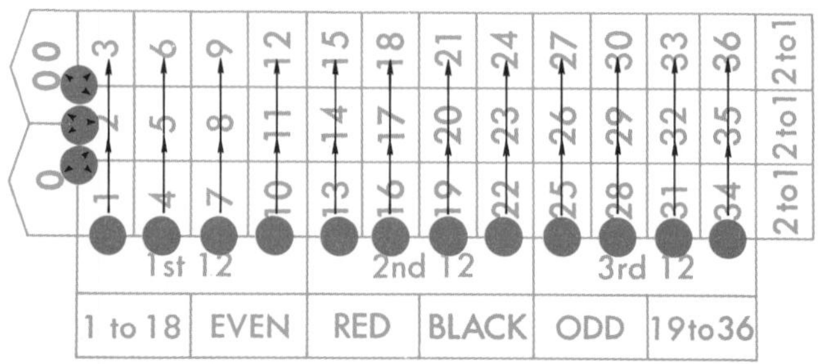

4 NUMBER BET PAYS 8 TO 1

00	3	6	9	12	15	18	21	24	27	30	33	36	2to1
	2	5	8	11	14	17	20	23	26	29	32	35	2to1
0	1	4	7	10	13	16	19	22	25	28	31	34	2to1
	1st 12				2nd 12				3rd 12				
	1 to 18		EVEN		RED		BLACK		ODD		19to36		

22 WAYS TO BET 4 NUMBERS

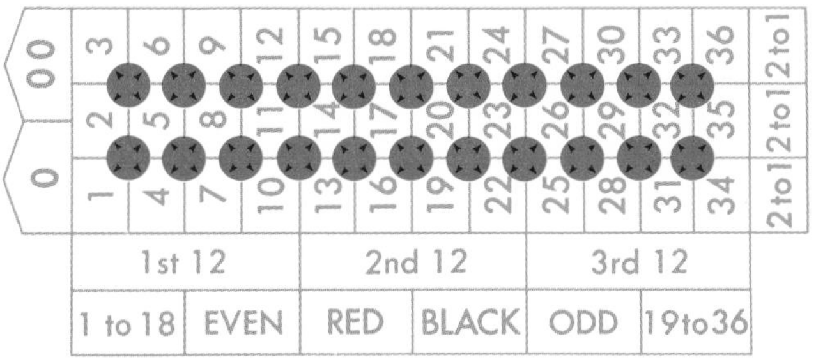

THE ONLY FIVE-NUMBER BET on the Roulette layout contains the following numbers: 0, 00, 1, 2, and 3 (see the FIVE-NUMBER BET diagram below). This particular bet should be avoided because it puts players at a 50 percent greater disadvantage than the other bets that have been or will be discussed in this section.

With this bet, players win 6 to 1. However, players will lose an average of 3 out of every 38 chips that are wagered; with every other bet, players will lose an average of only 2 out of every 38 of the chips they have wagered.

5 NUMBER BET
PAYS 6 TO 1

00	3	6	9	12	15	18	21	24	27	30	33	36	2to1
	2	5	8	11	14	17	20	23	26	29	32	35	2to1
0	1	4	7	10	13	16	19	22	25	28	31	34	2to1

1st 12		2nd 12		3rd 12	
1 to 18	EVEN	RED	BLACK	ODD	19to36

6 NUMBER BET
PAYS 5 TO 1

00	3	6	9	12	15	18	21	24	27	30	33	36	2to1
	2	5	8	11	14	17	20	23	26	29	32	35	2to1
0	1	4	7	10	13	16	19	22	25	28	31	34	2to1

1st 12		2nd 12		3rd 12	
1 to 18	EVEN	RED	BLACK	ODD	19to36

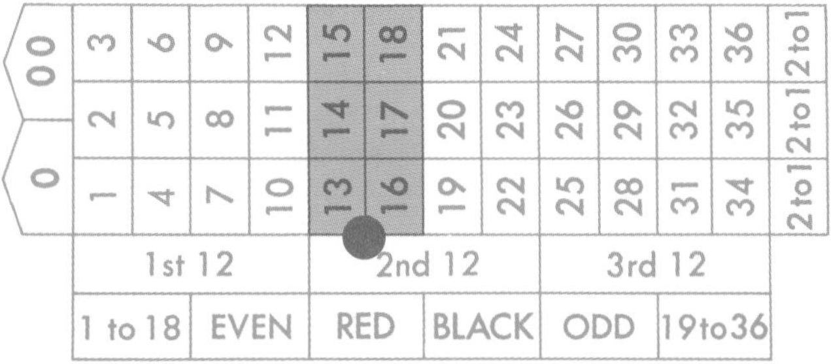

11 WAYS TO BET 6 NUMBERS

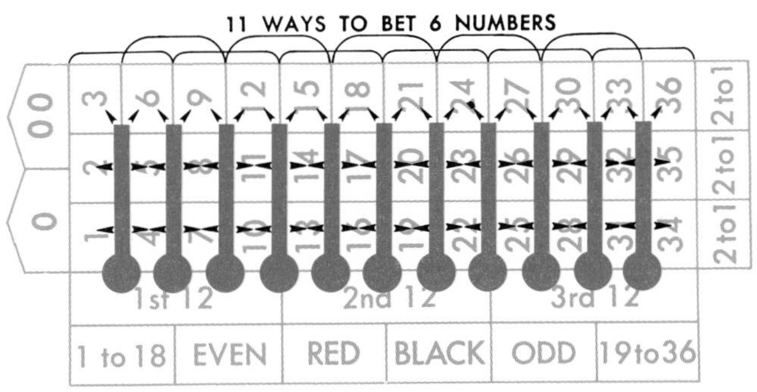

6 WAYS TO BET 12 NUMBERS
PAYS 2 TO 1

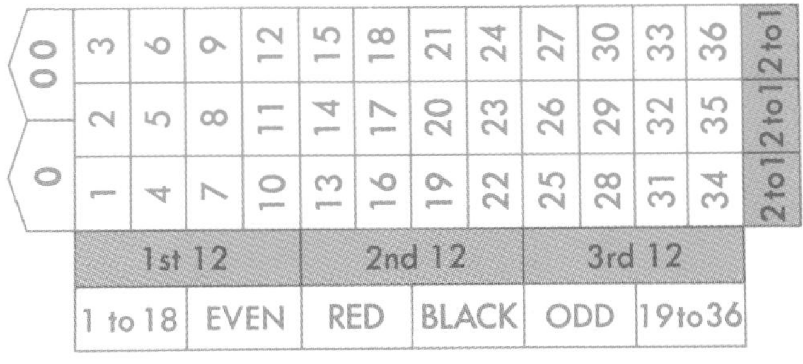

12 NUMBER COLUMN BET
PAYS 2 TO 1

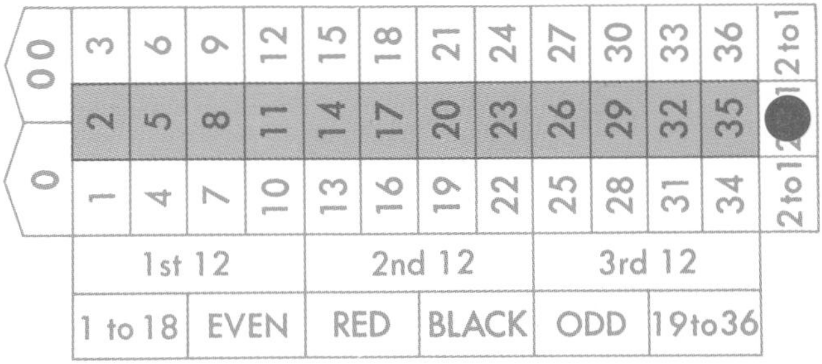

12 NUMBER DOZEN BET
PAYS 2 TO 1

0 00
3 6 9 12 15 18 21 24 27 30 33 36 2to1
2 5 8 11 14 17 20 23 26 29 32 35 2to1
1 4 7 10 13 16 19 22 25 28 31 34 2to1
1st 12 2nd 12 3rd 12
1 to 18 EVEN RED BLACK ODD 19to36

6 WAYS TO BET 18 NUMBERS
PAYS 1 TO 1

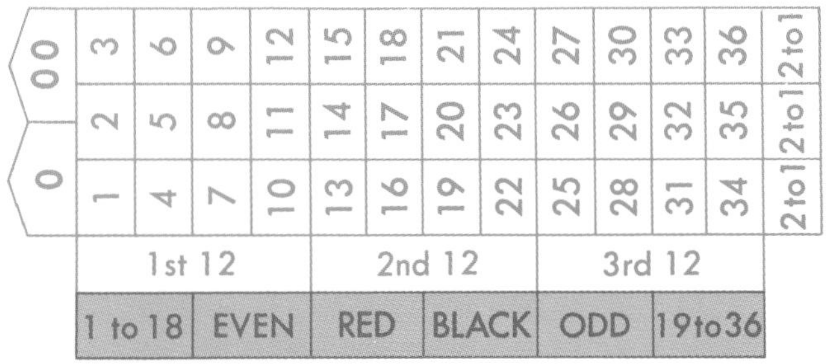

ALL OF THE LOW NUMBERS (1 through 18) or the high numbers (19 through 36) may be wagered. If the ball lands on a number from the chosen set, the player is paid 1 to 1.

ALL OF THE EVEN NUMBERS (those divisible by 2) or all of the odd numbers may be wagered. Both bets lose, just as all Outside Bets do, when the ball lands on either 0 or 00.

18 NUMBER HIGH AND LOW BETS
EACH PAYS 1 TO 1

00	3	6	9	12	15	18	21	24	27	30	33	36	2to1
	2	5	8	11	14	17	20	23	26	29	32	35	2to1
0	1	4	7	10	13	16	19	22	25	28	31	34	2to1
	1st 12				2nd 12				3rd 12				
	1 to 18		EVEN		RED		BLACK		ODD		19to36		

18 NUMBER EVEN AND ODD BETS
EACH PAYS 1 TO 1

00	3	6	9	12	15	18	21	24	27	30	33	36	2to1
	2	5	8	11	14	17	20	23	26	29	32	35	2to1
0	1	4	7	10	13	16	19	22	25	28	31	34	2to1
	1st 12				2nd 12				3rd 12				
	1 to 18		EVEN		RED		BLACK		ODD		19to36		

18 NUMBER RED AND BLACK BETS
EACH PAYS 1 TO 1

00	3	6	9	12	15	18	21	24	27	30	33	36	2to1
	2	5	8	11	14	17	20	23	26	29	32	35	2to1
0	1	4	7	10	13	16	19	22	25	28	31	34	2to1
	1st 12				2nd 12				3rd 12				
	1 to 18		EVEN		RED		BLACK		ODD		19to36		

PAYOFFS are made soon after the ball comes to rest in one of the pockets. The dealer first announces the winning number, places a marker on it, then sweeps in all of the losing wagers. Lastly, the winning wagers are paid off.

Outside wagers are paid off first, individually, in the bet spaces. Then the dealer calculates the total payoff for the winning Inside wagers and slides it across the table to directly in front of the player. All winning wagers and payoffs on Outside Bets remain on the layout for the next spin of the ball, unless the player removes them.

As soon as the dealer has paid off all the winning wagers, players may start wagering on the next spin of the ball. Wagering can continue until the dealer hears the ball hit the metal pockets, at which time he or she calls, "No more bets." Any bets made after this time are simply returned to the player.

The table minimum depends on the chip minimum. (Roulette tables have both a chip minimum and a table minimum.) A 25¢ chip minimum has a table minimum

PAYOFFS

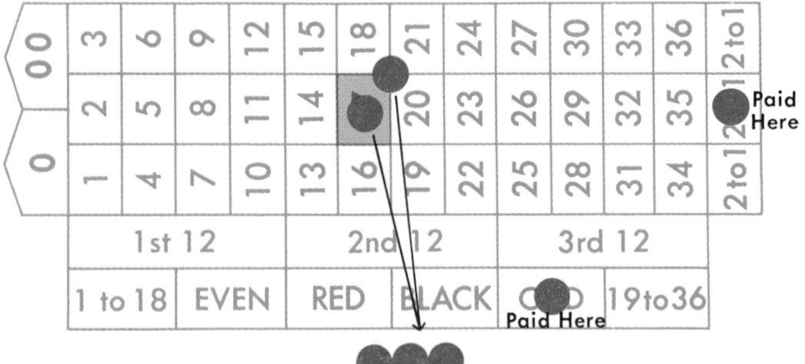

Dealer pointing to winning number

of $1, and a $1 chip minimum has a table minimum of $5. Each Outside Bet wagered must be at least the table minimum. On the six Outside Bets that pay 1 to 1, smaller casinos may have a $500 maximum, while major casinos can go as high as $10,000. Most casinos allow wagers half the size of this maximum on the six Outside Bets that pay 2 to 1.

OUTSIDE BETS

00	3	6	9	12	15	18	21	24	27	30	33	36	2to1
	2	5	8	11	14	17	20	23	26	29	32	35	2to1
0	1	4	7	10	13	16	19	22	25	28	31	34	2to1
	1st 12				2nd 12				3rd 12				
	1 to 18		EVEN		RED		BLACK		ODD		19to36		

INSIDE BETS

00	3	6	9	12	15	18	21	24	27	30	33	36	2to1
	2	5	8	11	14	17	20	23	26	29	32	35	2to1
0	1	4	7	10	13	16	19	22	25	28	31	34	2to1
	1st 12				2nd 12				3rd 12				
	1 to 18		EVEN		RED		BLACK		ODD		19to36		

INSIDE BETS also require at least the table minimum, but several different bets may be made with chips of lesser value totaling that amount. For example, when the table minimum is $1, four 25¢ chips may be used to create any combination of Inside Bets. Always ask the dealer what the table and chip minimums are. The maximum on any single Inside Bet is usually between $10 and $500, depending on the casino. Players may wager multiple Inside Bets of one through six numbers all containing the same number; but some casinos have a limit per player on the total payout from all Inside wagers. Casinos with low maximum limits often have a maximum Inside payoff limit of around $1,000.

THE CASINO ADVANTAGE for all bets except the single five-number bet is 5.26 percent because the casino will win on average 2 chips for every 38 wagered. For example, if a player wagers 1 chip on number 14 every spin, in a cycle of 38 spins that player will lose on 37 numbers and win 35 chips when number 14 appears. The casino would be ahead 2 chips.

The house advantage is the same for the other bets, all of which involve more numbers, because these pay off correspondingly smaller amounts of chips. For example, when wagering on a Split between the two numbers 14 and 17, a player loses on 36 numbers and wins 17 chips two times when the numbers 14 and 17 appear. The player wins only 34 chips while losing 36, and the casino would again be ahead 2 chips.

The same results can be worked out for every bet but the single five-number bet, where the player loses on 33 numbers and wins 6 chips five times when the numbers 0, 00, 1, 2, and 3 appear. Only 30 chips are won while 33 are lost, and the casino is ahead 3 chips. The casino wins 50 percent faster on this bet than on any of the others, and the house advantage is 7.89 percent.

EUROPEAN ROULETTE is played in most of the world's casinos. It also has thirty-six red and black numbers and a green 0 but not a green 00. Thus, the five-number bet combination is not possible. Also, the numbers on the European wheel are in a different order. The payoffs are the same in both games, but the casino advantage in the European game is only 2.70 percent compared to 5.26 percent in the American game. (Players lose on average 1 chip for every 37 wagered, not 2 chips for every 38 wagered.)

6 EN PRISON BETS

00	3	6	9	12	15	18	21	24	27	30	33	36	2to1
	2	5	8	11	14	17	20	23	26	29	32	35	2to1
0	1	4	7	10	13	16	19	22	25	28	31	34	2to1
	1st 12				2nd 12				3rd 12				
	1 to 18		EVEN		RED		BLACK		ODD		19to36		

WHEN THE "EN PRISON" BET IS OFFERED in European Roulette, the player loses only one half the wager when 0 appears; the house advantage is thus reduced to 1.35 percent. In a variation of the En Prison Bet, the player loses nothing when 0 appears. Instead, the dealer places the wager on the line bordering the bet, and the decision is made on the next spin. Even if the bet wins, though, the player wins back only the initial wager, which is equivalent to wagering half of it again.

In Atlantic City, the six Outside Bets that pay even money lose only half the wager if either 0 or 00 comes up. This is based on the En Prison rule. Since the casino wins 1 chip out of 38, its advantage is 2.63 percent, double that of the En Prison rule, but half of that in the other U.S. jurisdictions, which take the entire bet if either of the zeros hits.

HOUSE ADVANTAGE

NEVADA ROULETTE 0 and 00		**EUROPEAN ROULETTE** 0 only	
Five-Number Bet	**All Other Bets**	**En Prison Bets**	**All Other Bets**
7.89%	**5.26%**	**1.35%**	**2.70%**
Lose 3 of 38 Chips Bet	**Lose 2 of 38 Chips Bet**	**Lose 1 of 74 Chips Bet**	**Lose 1 of 37 Chips Bet**

ATLANTIC CITY ROULETTE

0 and 00

Lose 1 of 38 Chips Bet	**Outside 18-Number Bets**	**All Other Bets**	**Lose 2 of 38 Chips Bet**
	2.63%	**5.26%**	